DUCK STAMPS

DUCK STAMPS

Art in the Service of Conservation

SCOTT WEIDENSAUL

GALLERY BOOKS

This edition first published in the United States in 1989 by Gallery Books, an imprint of W.H. Smith Publishers, Inc., 112 Madison Avenue, New York 10016.

© Copyright: Dragon's World Ltd 1989
© Copyright: Text: Scott Weidensaul 1989

Published in England by Dragon's World Ltd., Limpsfield and London.

Designer: Ann Doolan
Editorial Assistant: Diana Steedman
Managing Editor: Pippa Rubinstein

Gallery Books are available for bulk purchase for sale promotions and premium use. For details write or telephone the Manager of Special Sales, W. H. Smith Publishers Inc., 112 Madison Avenue, New York, New York 10016. (212) 532-6600.

ISBN 0 8317 6381 7

Printed and bound in Spain by
GRUPO NERECAN - TONSA, San Sebastian

CONTENTS

Introduction

It is often said that carved duck decoys are America's only true folk art, just as jazz is its only native musical innovation. The makers of quilts may argue the point, but there is no doubt that North America's long tradition of waterfowling has left its mark artistically. Decoys that were once made for hard use in rugged conditions now fetch hundreds, even thousands of dollars, a situation that would have had the old carvers slack-jawed in amazement.

But long before decoy collecting became popular — back in the 1930s when many of those old stools were still in use — waterfowl hunters were buying federal duck stamps, a requirement for hunting. For a dollar or two, they got a gummed stamp somewhat larger than a postage stamp, decorated with an engraved image of ducks, geese or swans. Most hunters simply signed their stamps as the law required, and stuck it in their license holder. But others got hooked on collecting them. What started as a way to raise money for conservation soon became a hobby for thousands of people, who each year would buy a new, mint stamp and a print signed by the artist.

The appearance in the 1970s of state duck stamps lit the fuse, and in the past fifteen years, collecting these down-scaled works of art has experienced explosive growth. Each year, more than 20,000 signed, numbered prints of the federal design are sold, in addition to millions of stamps — many still bought by waterfowlers who through the years have, by their purchases, provided hundreds of millions of dollars for wetlands conservation. The same wellspring of funding is now being tapped by almost all of the states, as well as Canada and many private organizations, which issue stamps and prints of their own. Duck stamps are a multi-million dollar industry.

They are also art, a simple fact that sometimes gets lost in the shuffle. Reproduced here are many of the best examples, drawn from more than 50 years of state and federal designs. Within the small formats on which these works are painted, some of North America's best wildlife artists have captured the beauty and grace of our native waterfowl — a treasure at once enjoyed and preserved through duck stamps.

The Federal Duck Stamps

In 1934, the United States was reeling under the double blow of the Great Depression and Dust Bowl. The economy was near rock-bottom, and the nation had already suffered through five years of the worst drought in American history.

The human toll was bad enough, but wildlife was also devastated. All across the United States, wetlands that had traditionally nurtured millions of ducks and geese had gone dry and lake beds lay cracking in the oppressive sun. The climate wasn't the only culprit — people had recklessly drained prairie "pothole" marshes to create new farmland, then all but destroyed their farms through poor agricultural practices. The fall flights of waterfowl had dwindled to a trickle, leading many conservationists to fear that, without immediate human intervention, the birds might never recover.

The biggest problem was money. With so many people living in destitution, it was difficult for the government to allocate funds for birds. President Franklin D. Roosevelt was sympathetic, at least in words, but would not release emergency funds for waterfowl conservation, despite the best efforts of his director of the Bureau of Biological Survey, J. N. "Ding" Darling.

Darling was a respected political cartoonist from Iowa, a staunch conservative who took the post despite his misgivings about Roosevelt's policies, and — most of all — a fiery conservationist who used his nationally syndicated cartoons to champion wise resource use. In early 1934 he had served on a presidential commission charged with drawing up a plan to save the nation's waterfowl, and when Roosevelt called him to take charge of the Biological Survey

Frank W. Benson, renowned for his etchings, was commissioned to do the 1935–36 federal stamp. Both the stamp and the larger print are exceedingly valuable to collectors because they are the rarest in a long series.

Previous page Two mallards, moments from impact, settle onto a marshy backwater in "Mallards Dropping In," J. N. "Ding" Darling's design for the first federal duck stamp. Darling, a famous cartoonist, was the chief of the U.S. Biological Survey at the time he designed the stamp.

The 1940–41 federal stamp (top) was graced with a pair of black ducks painted by Francis Lee Jaques — perhaps the first of the "classic" duck stamp designs, and the first to feature black ducks, (right), now a declining species in the East, Joseph Knap, whose 1937–38 stamp (above) depicted greater scaup, was the first to issue prints of his design.

Better known for his murals than his
wildlife art, Alden Ripley designed the
1942–43 stamp (top) that shows a trio
of American wigeon. Also called
baldpates because of their white
foreheads, wigeon (left) are found
across most of North America as
migrants, breeders or wintering birds.
The 1939–40 stamp (above) by Lynn
Bogue Hunt Sr, focused on green-
winged teal.

Illustrator Walter A. Weber filled the frame of his 1944–45 design with three white-fronted geese (above), while Robert Hines — who later directed the duck stamp program — chose a flock of redheads as the subject of his 1946–47 effort (opposite).

(the forerunner of the U.S. Fish and Wildlife Service), Darling saw it as a sterling opportunity to put his views into action.

Darling is frequently credited with creating the federal duck stamp, but in reality, the idea was around for several years before he came to Washington. Private hunting organizations were lobbying Congress with different ways to pay for waterfowl preservation — by levying taxes on ammunition, for example. The American Game Protective Association backed a federal revenue stamp that would function as a license, and it was that plan that received the support of a special Senate committee that was studying the matter in 1932.

The Migratory Bird Hunting Stamp Act was passed by Congress March 16, 1934, at the same time Darling was appointed chief of the Biological Survey. The creation of the duck stamp held the promise of money to fund desperately needed waterfowl conservation projects, but Darling felt the need was more immediate. President Roosevelt had shrugged off his requests for money, so when the duck stamp bill came up for a vote, Darling engineered a masterful end-run, using an unknowing Congress to pull a fast one on the President.

As contributing authors Philip A. Du Mont and Henry Reeves
relate in the U.S. Fish and Wildlife Service book *Flyways*, Darling
enlisted an ally for the ruse:

"The vote on the ... Act was underway when Senator Peter
Norbeck of South Dakota rose to ask unanimous approval for a rider
to be added to the bill. Senator Norbeck, who had a reputation as a
dedicated conservationist, pulled from his pocket a piece of paper on
which he had written his resolution. As Ding told the story later, on
that morning Senator Norbeck had left his upper plate on the table in
the washroom because of a slight gum infection, and that, together
with his emulsified Swedish and English diction, made it impossible
for anyone to understand him.

"But because of his long record of integrity, the Senate voted
unanimously to accept his resolution. The President was preparing
for a fishing trip when the bill reached him for his signature. He read
the title but not the amendment and signed the bill."

Another three weeks passed before an aide noticed that Norbeck's
unintelligible plea to the Senate had neatly slipped an additional $6

Another of Walter A. Weber's federal designs, the 1950–51 stamp bore two trumpeter swans flying above Red Rock Lakes National Wildlife Refuge in Montana, where this magnificent bird was saved from possible extinction.

"Early Express," Clayton B. Seager's
dynamic 1953–54 painting, shows a
flock of blue-winged teal flaring
sharply into the wind.

million to the Biological Survey for duck conservation. Roosevelt, admiring a slick political maneuver even at his own expense, congratulated Darling on the move. That $6 million was the nest egg, with the duck stamp money to follow.

A Beginning

The first stamp was issued in August, 1934. The design was an ink wash by Darling himself, and showed two mallards dropping happily — it is the only word for the birds' expressions — into a marsh. Darling later said the design was from a preliminary sketch, one of several he'd done for a meeting with the Bureau of Engraving. Darling was given the opportunity to purchase the very first $1 stamp. There was no print, because no one foresaw that duck stamps would become such a popular collector's item. The only purpose, in those early years, was to raise money for waterfowl.

Roughly 635,000 of Darling's inaugural stamps were sold. By 1938 sales topped one million, and a print was available through the artist — a practice that Joseph Knap had begun the year before. Darling and the two other earliest artists, bowing to the clamor of fledgling

Gadwalls are common dabbling ducks over much of the United States and Canada, but because they are rather plain (the white wing speculum is the only real field mark) they are rarely shown on duck stamps. Maynard Reece's 1951–52 design is the only federal stamp to feature this species.

collectors, also redid their designs in a larger format for release as prints. Then, as now, the prints were a privately arranged sideline to the duck stamp, and not a government-administered sale: the artist receives nothing from the government, but retains the right to market his design. The prints and stamps did not always jibe, because each was produced from a different piece of artwork — a practice known as "repainting" still followed by many stamp artists today, although they are more careful to copy their winning design exactly. Darling's 1934–5 stamp and print are an excellent example of the disparity between many of the early stamps and prints; the hen's feet hang limp in the stamp, but are flared for impact in the print, and there are a number of other changes in position and plumage between the two. And while the stamp art was done in ink wash, the print was based on an etching.

In the beginning, the duck stamp program was a loosely organized affair. The artists were commissioned to produce the artwork, although "commission" may be too formal a term for so unstructured (and unpaid) an arrangement. By the late 1930s and early 1940s, the program had expanded to a contest, in a very limited sense; several artists were invited to submit designs, from which the U.S. Fish and Wildlife Service chose the stamp.

One of the most unusual federal designs was Edward Bierly's common merganser pair on the 1956–57 stamp. The leafless, reflected tree and somber tone of the work seem more in keeping with a Halloween illustration than a duck stamp, and lend an otherworldly effect to this dramatic piece.

Maynard Reece, who has won the federal duck stamp contest an unmatched five times, was also at the center of controversy for his 1959–60 design "King Buck" (above); the painting of a Labrador retriever with a dead mallard offended many non-hunters. Reece's 1969–70 painting of two white-winged scoters (right) was more typical of most duck stamps, and was the last federal issue in black-and-white.

The second design, a trio of canvasbacks by Frank W. Benson, is unusual in that the tiny stamp exhibits more detail than the larger print that Benson later produced. This paradox is due in large part to the mediums used — watercolor for the stamp art, which government engravers then converted to line for the plate, and an etching from which the print was made. Benson was renowned for his roughly rendered etchings, and his duck stamp print was a fine example of his loose, almost jagged style. His 1935–36 print is also by far the rarest and costliest of the federal series, as is the stamp, which was printed in rose-red ink. Only about 100 Benson prints were made, and by most counts, little more than half have survived to this point, commanding thousands of dollars from collectors.

Glory Days

Many of the best artists of the day were enlisted to do duck stamps in the years before and immediately after World War II — men like Francis Lee Jaques (1940–41), the famous illustrator whose back-

Soft lighting wraps a pair of Ross' geese in the 1970–71 painting by Edward Bierly, the first to be painted and reproduced in color.

Some of the most unusual waterfowl in the United States have been featured on the federal duck stamp over the years. The endangered nene, or Hawaiian goose on the 1964–65 issue by Stanley Stearns (right); the oldsquaw, an arctic species, on the 1967–68 by Les Kouba (below); and the beautiful hooded merganser on Claremont Gale Pritchard's 1968–69 design (opposite).

ground paintings brought many museum habitat groups to life; Lynn Bogue Hunt Sr, (1939–40), well-known for his illustrations of hunting and fishing scenes, and Alden L. Ripley (1942–43), whose watercolors and murals had won him acclaim from the art world. In many cases, these men were not "wildlife artists" in the confining sense that the term is used today, and they certainly were not duck stamp specialists, as so many winning artists are now.

Of the first twenty federal designs, some, like Knap's 1937–38 scaup and Roland Clark's 1938–39 pintail pair, show a stilted awkwardness reminiscent of many nineteenth century sporting prints — not surprising, since the artists worked in that school of art most of their life. In Jaques' black duck design of 1940–41, however, can be seen the first of the "classic" duck stamp compositions and treatments. The two blacks are flying low, just skimming the tops of the reeds. The birds are rendered crisply, and the proportions are almost perfect — a reflection of Jaques' lifelong infatuation with waterfowl. The print, a stone lithograph, takes the attention to detail and composition even further, and the result is a gem.

Compared to modern designs, the early federal stamps incorporated a wide range of styles and approaches. The 1943–44 design, a

A goose hunter sets out decoys in the tidewater of Maryland's Eastern Shore, an area rich in waterfowling tradition. By law, every waterfowl hunter must buy a federal duck stamp as a form of license — purchases which account for much of the annual stamp sales.

drypoint etching by Walter Bohl, features a pair of flying wood ducks against an almost blank sky. The very next year, scientific illustrator Walter A. Weber filled the stamp with the closely cropped images of three white-fronted geese, dropping almost straight toward the viewer. Six years later, Weber again captured the duck stamp honors, this time in open competition, with a striking painting of trumpeter swans in flight.

Bob Hines brought his fluid use of line to the stamp program with a 1946–47 stamp and print showing a flock of redheads, with a drake just about to land. Emblematic of those less-formal days, Hines' first attempt was returned by the U.S. Fish and Wildlife Service, with a request to take out a second flock of ducks that he had included. The very next year Hines was hired to administer the stamp program, a post he held for thirty-two years.

Hines oversaw the dramatic surge in interest in duck stamps, both by collectors and by artists, and the growth of what remains the federal government's only art contest. The competition for the 1949–50 stamp attracted eight entries, including some by invitation. The following year, 65 artists tried; the year after that, 51, with a number submitting more than one design. Most official histories of the federal duck stamp program list the 1949 contest as the first open competition, but Maynard Reece, who designed the 1948–49 stamp issued the year before, places the start of the contest several years earlier:

"They did not have a full-fledged, open competition, but I was never invited to send in anything — and I sent in one or two years before I won anything.... As far as I'm concerned, it was a competition. It may not have been the same type as they have now, but it was competition. There were many designs in there, and they were judged, and sometimes I'd get second and third," he said.

Reece, who was working for a publishing house in Des Moines at the time, found out about the duck stamp contest after being introduced to fellow Iowan "Ding" Darling. "I was a hunter, of course, and I knew what the stamp was, but I knew nothing about the design," he said, until a mutual friend set up a meeting between the two men. His first stamp showed three buffleheads skimming the waves.

"When I did my first stamp, I got $6 (per print) if I sold it to Abercrombie & Fitch, who were handling it for the publisher, and if the publisher sold it themselves — they were selling to other galleries — I got $7.50. They were selling the prints for $15 a piece," Reece said, "and we had 'big' editions of maybe two or three hundred. We didn't even bother numbering them. We had no idea of the popularity that would occur."

One of the finest stamps to come out of this early period was the twentieth stamp, Clayton Seager's 1953–54 design, "Early Express." Like Jaques' earlier black ducks, Seager's design juxtapositions flying birds against marshland foliage. Five blue-winged teal, banking sharply to the left, are frozen as they turn to escape. Bulrush fronds, bent by a strong wind, lean hard in the same direction, intensifying the feeling of motion. The composition is intricate, especially considering the limited format.

An almost Oriental feeling pervades Edward J. Bierly's painting of

Besting more than 200 competitors,
Arthur Cook won the contest for the
1972–73 federal stamp with his
watercolor of two emperor geese. Little
known in the Lower 48, emperors are
related to snow geese, and breed only
in Alaska.

Wood ducks climb into the air in an oil by David Maass from which the 1974–75 stamp was made. Maass, who won the federal contest again in the 1980s, has built on his duck stamp wins to establish himself as a major force in waterfowl art.

Another Alaskan specialty, the Stellar's eider is one of the most unusually patterned of North American ducks. This painting, by Lee LeBlanc, won the contest for the 1973–74 stamp.

two common (then known as American) mergansers from the 1956–57 stamp. The birds are depicted flying low over glassy, still water that perfectly reflects a bare tree in the background. The mood is somber and surrealistic, a world apart from previous designs.

Also a world apart was Reece's 1959–60 design "King Buck," which featured as its main subject a portrait of a champion black Labrador retriever, holding a dead mallard in its mouth.

"They decided in Washington that they should introduce a conservation project to prove that retrieving dogs were really benefiting wildlife because they were saving ducks that would otherwise be lost," Reece recalled recently. "So that year it was decided that they would use a retrieving dog on the stamp — everybody knew that. I had not entered in a few years — in fact, I dropped out after 1948 and didn't enter again until 1951, dropped after 1951 and entered again in 1959."

Reece might not have entered even then, except that he received a telephone call from Nilo Farms, owned by the Winchester firearms company. They, too, had heard about the duck stamp office's plan to feature a retriever on the upcoming stamp, and they thought Reece might be interested in painting their national field champion, King

A rule change followed Delaware native James Fisher's win of the 1975–76 federal contest with a painting of a canvasback decoy (below). Beautiful and unusual, the design nevertheless raised the hackles of many other artists, and the duck stamp office responded by requiring that live waterfowl be the subjects for all future entries. Canvasbacks were earlier featured on the 1965–66 federal stamp by Ron Jenkins (left).

James P. Fisher

Buck. Reece visited Nilo Farms, sketched the dog and won with his wash and gouache painting.

The painting, which beat more than 100 other entries, generated a small storm of protest. "Some people were saying it was horrible, with a dead duck in its mouth. On the flip side of the coin, there were a great number of dog lovers that said 'This is wonderful — at last we have something to show what a great thing retrieving dogs are.' So it all balanced itself out," Reece said. Actually, it more than balanced itself out — the print was one of the most popular of the early federal series.

Between 1948 and 1971, Reece accomplished the incredible by winning the federal contest five times, a feat no other artist has even approached. His first, the buffleheads on the 1948–49 stamp, is rather stiff and artificial, as is his 1951–52 effort, showing a pair of gadwalls springing from the water. There is a much greater sense of life in Reece's last two designs — a pair of white-winged scoters running across the surface to get airborne, on the 1969–70 stamp, and three cinnamon teal for the 1971–72 edition. It is evident in these paintings that the artist had hit his stride.

The boldest departure from the norm in the history of the federal duck stamp contest, Alderson Magee's exquisitely rendered scratchboard of a family of Canada geese won the competition for the 1976–77 stamp. Canada geese are, with mallards, the most successful waterfowl on the continent, found in virtually every state and province.

Color, and Growing Popularity

The federal program took a giant leap toward its current level of popularity with the 1970–71 stamp, when, for the first time, the stamp and print were issued in full color. Edward Bierly, who had won the contest twice before, took the top slot with a watercolor of two Ross' geese, an uncommon bird that looks like a tiny snow goose. The birds in Bierly's painting are standing in shallow water; the nearer goose is preening, and has one wing fully extended. The lighting and color are beautiful, although there is a confusing use of shadow and reflection in the background. Still, Bierly's painting stands as one of the finest from the duck stamp program's middle years.

The color photolithography used to produce prints of Bierly's painting gave collectors a far more attractive product than had been possible with the black-and-white stone lithography or etchings of earlier years. The result was predictable. Print sales began to climb quickly: 700 of the Ross' goose prints sold, bringing Bierly about $50,000, while Lee LeBlanc, the artist of the 1973–74 design, sold nearly 1,900 numbered prints. Many observers point to 1974, when

A male hooded merganser slides across a reflective lake in Albert Earl Gilbert's 1978–79 design. Gilbert was the first duck stamp artist to remarque some of his prints in color — a trend now abandoned on the federal level, but popular among state programs.

Ross' geese were featured on the federal 1977–78 stamp, the second appearance in less than ten years for this rare western goose. The acrylic original, by Martin Murk, was 5-by-7-inches, the standard size of federal entries until recently, when it was increased to 8-by-10-inches.

Eye-level with its subjects, Lawrence "Ken" Michaelson's 1979–80 stamp gives the viewer a close-up of a green-winged teal pair. This same format, a closely cropped composition of two birds on the water, had won for Michaelson the year before in California, although in that case the subjects were hooded mergansers.

David Maass won with an attractive pair of wood ducks, as the real beginning of the print collecting bonanza. Maass, who has since become one of the premier waterfowl artists in the country, sold 2,700 prints; by the time he won the contest again, in 1982, demand was such that more than 23,000 prints were issued.

Two of the most unusual federal designs came back-to-back in the mid 1970s. James P. Fisher, a first-time contest entrant, won the 1975–76 competition with a painting of an old, weather-beaten canvasback decoy, wrapped in its anchor cord with a vignette of three flying cans in the upper corner. The painting created a storm that was, in many ways, reminiscent of the controversy fifteen years earlier over Maynard Reece's Labrador painting, with many contending that a decoy had no place on the duck stamp. To avoid a repeat, the duck stamp office in the U.S. Fish and Wildlife Service quickly amended the rules to insure that a live duck, goose or swan was the main subject of all future stamps. The Service also eliminated "prejudging" by the duck stamp office after an allegation — never proven — that Fisher's win was rigged.

The next year's winner stands as one of the most dramatic — and unusual — designs to come out of federal program. Using scratch-

*Ruddy ducks belong to a group known
as "stiff-tailed" ducks — an apt name,
as shown in two federal stamps. John
S. Wilson's 1981–82 effort (above)
shows a white-cheeked male with his
mate, while the 1941–42 stamp by
Edwin R. Kalmbach depicts a family
on their prairie marsh breeding
grounds.*

27

board, Connecticut artist Alderson Magee created a stunning, monochromatic scene showing a pair of Canada geese guarding their four chicks. Scratched through a layer of ink to a ceramic-coated surface below, Magee's work is crisp and bold, perfectly suited to the hard-edged feathers and strongly contrasting plumage of the adults, while not losing the downiness of the goslings. What is even more amazing is that Magee did the drawing in just three days, submitting it less than half an hour before the deadline.

Where Magee's design showed a superb sense of line and value, Al Gilbert's hooded merganser (1978–79) showed an equal mastery of color and composition. With its fan-shaped crest of black and white, a hooded merganser drake is a difficult subject for an artist to handle without making the bird look ridiculous, but Gilbert's opaque watercolor avoids that trap. The drake is gliding across smooth, blue water, painted flat with only a few white highlights to denote ripples.

The Explosion

Oddly, one of the events that had the greatest impact on the federal duck stamp contest in the 1970s had nothing to do with print sales or

Strong side-lighting and threatening clouds make David Maass' 1982–83 design one of the best of recent federal stamps. The featured subject of this oil, canvasbacks, have greatly declined in numbers in the past twenty years, due to drought and habitat loss, at a time when their popularity on duck stamps has risen just as sharply.

competition rules. It was an article in *National Wildlife* magazine, the publication of the National Wildlife Federation. In 1978, the magazine ran a story titled "The World's Richest Art Competition?" that focused on the big profits that federal winners were earning. Newspapers and other magazines followed with stories of their own. Artists, professionals and amateurs alike, figured that with a possible million-dollar payoff, they had nothing to loose. The stampede was on.

When Lawrence Michaelson won the 1979–80 contest with a closeup of two, swimming, green-winged teal, he competed against 373 other paintings. Just two years later, the field had ballooned to more than 2,000 submissions, ranging from the sublime (like winner David Maass' stormy canvasback oil) to the ridiculous. The federal employees who organize the duck stamp contest like to tell stories about the Donald Ducks they got, about the childish drawings and bizarre doodles that showed up in the mail before the contest.

Much of that ended in 1983 when, for the first time, the government imposed at $20 entrance fee on all paintings — a levy later raised to $35, then to $50, in an effort to restrict the contest to only those artists truly serious about entering. From the high of 2,099

With publicity about the federal stamp contest (and the high profits that winning artists were earning), the field of entrants burgeoned in the early 1980s. In the 1979–80 contest, about 370 artist entered; the next year, when this acrylic of two mallards by Richard Plasschaert won, the judges sifted more than 1,300 paintings before making their decision.

Refuges: Havens for All

The money spent on federal duck stamps supports, in large part, the National Wildlife Refuge (NWR) system. Although many refuges were established primarily for waterfowl, they protect valuable wetlands and the myriad other creatures that rely on these fragile ecosystems. Clockwise: A female snapping turtle lumbers up a sunny bank at Bombay Hook NWR in Delaware, ready to lay her eggs in the warm ground; a northern mockingbird finds a convenient perch at Chincoteague NWR in Virginia; white pelicans cruise beneath snow-touched hills in Montana's Red Rock Lakes NWR, established to save the trumpeter swan; snow geese feed along the beach at the Brigantine unit of Forsythe NWR in New Jersey, with the Atlantic City skyline in the distance; and a great egret silently stalks a quiet backwater, alert to the chance for fish or frogs.

in 1981, the number of entrants has dropped steadily, down to 681 in the 1989–90 contest, held in the fall of 1988.

In recent years, the duck stamp office has instituted a number of other important changes. After more than 50 years, nine species of North American waterfowl had still never been featured on a stamp — the lesser scaup, spectacled eider, king eider, red-breasted merganser, Barrow's goldeneye, black-bellied whistling duck, mottled duck, black scoter and surf scoter. To rectify that omission, the government announced that beginning with the 1988–89 contest, only certain species would be eligible each year, insuring more even coverage. That year, the five permissible subjects were spectacled eider, red-breasted merganser, Barrow's goldeneye, black-bellied whistling duck and lesser scaup; a pair of the last graced Nebraska artist Neal R. Anderson's winning gouache.

"We will continue to do an elimination process, until we eventually come to the point where we have less than five species left," said Norma Opgrand, who heads the duck stamp office for the U.S. Fish and Wildlife Service. "Then we'll just have four species eligible for the contest, then three, then two." If all goes according to plan, by the 1996 contest only the last undone species with be eligible — something many artists wish would be the case sooner, believing that by restricting the contest in any given year to only one kind of waterfowl, the judging would be easier, and perhaps fairer. It's a point Opgrand concedes, and is one of the reasons for the gradual move in that direction. "There are probably a hundred excellent paintings each year, and it's much more difficult to say 'This Canada goose is better than that mallard or this snow goose or that redhead.' You'll be comparing apples to apples."

Judging

Even with more restrictive rules, the field remains a big one each year, and many artists, even some that enter faithfully, view it almost as a crap shoot. The judging, once a single-day affair, now covers three days.

The five judges are selected to give a balance to the panel; in 1988, they included the editor of *Sports Afield* magazine, himself an artist; an art educator; renowned wildlife artist Bob Kuhn; a Ducks Unlimited member who collects wildlife art; and the executive director of the Izaak Walton League. The contest traditionally starts on a Monday morning in early November. In years past, the judges got their first look at the art the morning of the competition, but that, too, has changed.

"We bring the judges in the day before the contest starts and we have a formal briefing for them," Opgrand explained. "We walk them through the whole procedure, even to the point of having them sit in the chairs they'll be seated in. Sunday evening they are given as much time as they want to preview the artwork — if they want to stay there until midnight, examining and previewing the art, they can. They can discuss the art (among themselves) in a very generic sense — they can't say 'This is clearly the winner.' They might say 'That's an interesting way the light's coming through the wings

An almost gauzy quality to the light marks Phil Scholer's 1983–84 acrylic of two pintails.

there,' or 'The color on this water is similar to what I've seen when I've been out on the Chesapeake.' We actually discourage any conversation among the judges."

Only those pieces that are in violation of the contest's rules are removed before the judges are brought in. "We always get people that forget to read the rules, or forget what they've read," Opgrand said. "That's the only purging we do, unless a drawing is so far afield that it's not a recognizable species. Sometimes we get some *very* strange things — somebody submitted a painting of a single feather as an entry one year. It was really a waste of $50, because the rules are very specific that it has to be a live species that's drawn." Even those that abide by the regulations display a wide range of talent, she said. "Out of 800 or 900 entries there's a lot of junk, but part of the reason for this is that the contest is open to everyone. I think that's a very American thing, that anyone who wants to enter can do it. As a federal agency, I think that it's nice we don't restrict it."

The day of the contest, the judges have two more hours to review the paintings before the first round begins. In this preliminary session, every submission is considered, with the panel voting individually to keep it or take it out of the running, on a simple majority vote. Nevertheless, the first round usually takes all day, and may spill into the second. As a contest worker displays a painting before a judge, a photograph of it is shown on a large screen for the audience, and on two monitors for the rest of the panel. Judges can linger over each entry as long as they like, taking their time with their decision. At the end of the round, each judge is given the chance to go back to the rejected entries and retrieve up to five each that would be carried over to the second round. In 1988 (judging for the 1989–90 stamp), the judges sent thirty-nine entries to the second round.

In the second, and subsequent, rounds, voting is done numerically. Like Olympic judges ranking a high-dive, they assign each painting a score from one to ten; the high and low scores are thrown out, and the middle three added together. At the end of the second round, paintings with the top five scores move on. This usually means about twenty pieces, because many have tied scores; in 1988, however, the total was only thirteen.

The third round is a repeat of the second — but at a much higher level of tension for the judges, and especially for any artists in the

American brant — now considered the same species as the western black brant — were chosen by artist Edward Bierly for his 1963–64 painting. The distant lighthouse evokes the Mid-Atlantic coast, where this small goose winters in large numbers.

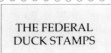

audience whose art is in the finals. At the end of the third round, if there are three paintings ranked one, two and three numerically, the winner is declared. Otherwise, the tied entries are scored yet again. "It's a very difficult process on the judges," Opgrand said.

Winning the contest can mean fame and fortune for the lucky artist, but to be selected a judge is also a mark of pride. Pennsylvania outdoor writer Sylvia Bashline was among five judges in the 1978–79 contest that eventually selected Al Gilbert's hooded merganser, an experience she still values more than a decade later.

"I wanted to do it as soon as they called me — it was 'Oh, of course, who wouldn't?' I was very anxious to do it, but there is no way to bone up for something like that. You either know it, or you don't." Bashline was only the second woman asked to judge what had traditionally been a male-dominated field, another, though minor, reason for her enthusiasm.

The judging was then a single-day affair. Bashline flew from Pennsylvania to Washington the morning of the judging, and went straight into an exhaustive briefing by duck stamp office personnel.

William C. Morris' wigeon pair captured the top spot for the 1984–85 stamp, the 50th anniversary of the federal program — a fact highlighted on the stamp itself. Oddly, Morris' painting did not include the drake's delicate vermiculations, the fine, closely spaced lines on the flank and shoulder feathers that this species usually displays.

"They thoroughly, thoroughly brief you before you start, on everything. They brief you on how the paintings have to stand up to being reduced, the engraving of them and what you have to look for to know if they'll engrave well. They brief you on what's been selected in the past, and of course on the regulations.

"They have experts there for you to talk to if you need them — experts in engraving, in art and wildlife. If you don't know if that's the way a particular duck should look, you can ask. They won't offer, but you can ask 'Is that tail feather right?' And then the expert will say, 'Yes, it's perfect,' or 'No, it's not.' And everybody hears that, all the judges. The experts are there for you to use if you wish, but they don't insert themselves, which is very helpful."

The year Bashline judged, about 300 paintings had been entered — a tiny field by recent standards, but a daunting prospect for the judges.

"In the audience behind you you may have the artists, their families — any number of people may be sitting in the darkened auditorium behind you," Bashline recalled. "You are very quiet in your comments (during the prejudging), but when it gets down to the real judging, you have to hold up your cards and everyone can

Representative of the photographic style now in vogue among duck stamp artists and judges, Gerald Mobley's 1985–86 painting shows a drake cinnamon teal in exquisite detail. The use of one or two birds that fill the painting, most artists believe, adds to an entry's impact, and thus its chance of winning.

BURTON E. MOORE, JUNR. ©1986

see. It's terribly tense, and you hope you are in line with the other judges.

"It's long and drawn-out, and really an awesome responsibility, when you know that you could make someone a millionaire. When you get down to the last five you know that all of them would make a great duck stamp. The importance is what you're doing to the artist."

Once the judges' selection is made, the winning painting goes on a whirlwind tour — to major waterfowl festivals in Maryland and California with many of the other top entries, then to the Bureau of Engraving in December for creation of the stamp. "The engravers engrave the design on a metal plate, directly from the art," Opgrand said. "They're not using the computerized method of engraving." Before the plate is made, however, a design and modeling team from the Bureau of Engraving creates one or more mockups of the finished stamp, showing the typeface and the position of the inscription; the U.S. Fish and Wildlife Service has a chance to review the design before the stamp is actually made.

Painted flatly, with a high degree of stylization in the water, Burton E. Moore Jr.'s fulvous whistling-duck has a sharpness that makes it one of the most striking of federal designs. It was the basis for the 1986–87 stamp and print.

A New Sophistication

With the 1980s, duck stamps reached their most sophisticated level, both as an art form and a collectible. The 1986–87 design by Burton E. Moore Jr. reflects as well on the contest's judging as on the artist. An acrylic of a fulvous whistling-duck, the painting is a curious mix of detail and pure design that has much in common with Gilbert's merganser. This was the first time the fulvous whistling-duck, a rare Gulf Coast resident, had appeared in the federal series — a fact that print promoters were quick to capitalize on by pushing the edition as a "first of species," similar to the popular "first of state" prints.

The 1983–84 stamp — two pintails by Phil Scholer — used strong backlighting to show the smooth planes of the birds' bodies, and set off a stampede of other artists using the same soft lighting in their work. It, like the following stamp, a pair of wigeon by William C. Morris, focused tightly on a pair of swimming ducks, the quintessential duck stamp combination. Each is handled very differently, though, proving that originality can lift the commonplace to new heights.

The quality has not, unfortunately, been universally high in recent

White-capped waves on a windy marsh add a feeling of motion to Arthur G. Anderson's 1987–88 painting of three redheads.

Eight downy chicks and their mother are the subjects of "Nine Mallards," Edward A. Morris' 1961–62 federal design. The first edition of the print consisted of 250; today, federal winners issue roughly 20,000 signed, numbered prints — testament to the mushrooming popularity of collecting.

years. The 1981–82 design, a pair of ruddy ducks by John S. Wilson, is a dull, rather shallow painting. There is no attempt at habitat or depth — the birds and their reflection seem to be pasted against a flat, toned background, and there is a cartoon-like feel to it. The 1987–88 stamp by Arthur G. Anderson has good movement in its three redheads sailing in low over a choppy lake, but suffers from poor handling of the color — the shadows are heavy and black, especially on the heads of the drakes and the hen's breast.

Arguably the finest federal design in twenty years, however, was Daniel Smith's 1988–9 work. A lone snow goose is shown flying low over a lake at sunrise, as the mist burns off the water, partially obscuring the distant shoreline. The bird is backlit, throwing most of its body into cool shadow while illuminating the secondaries of one open wing. Light curves over the top of the other wing, touching the shoulder and the edges of the flexed primaries. A rich golden-yellow suffuses the painting, giving it a sense of place and atmosphere missing from most designs — a feeling accentuated by the bird's presence in the middle ground, rather than tight in the foreground, as most modern stamp designs have been.

The paintings by both Arthur Anderson and Dan Smith conformed to a request the duck stamp office had made to its judges, starting in 1986: pick designs with motion, action and a feeling of life, preferably of ducks in flight. In November of 1988, however, the panel picking the 1989–90 design overrode that suggestion, choosing Neal R. Anderson's pair of lesser scaup, which are depicted as swimming across the surface of a smooth, misty pond. While well-executed, Anderson's painting lacks the originality of Smith's effort, or of Moore's whistling-duck.

With all the hype over contests and editions, first of species prints and the arcane of judging, it is easy to lose sight of the federal duck

A standout in more than half a century of duck stamp art, Daniel Smith's 1988–89 painting of a lone snow goose flying through the backlit mist of morning has tremendous impact and a fine sense of place.

stamp's most important purpose — wetlands and waterfowl conservation. The stamp program, it can be argued, is one of the most successful tools the government has ever devised for raising money for conservation. From the $1 originally charged in 1934, the face price of a federal stamp has increased swiftly in recent years, from $5 to $7.50 in 1979, to $10 in 1987 and $12.50 in 1989. Each year, millions are sold — to waterfowl hunters who sign them and carry them afield as a form of license, to collectors eager to expand their hobby, to bird-watchers and others who want to contribute to conservation work. Over the years, more than $350 million has been raised specifically to save wetlands and the wildlife, including ducks and geese, that rely on them. In all, more than four million acres have been preserved — much through the National Wildlife Refuge System. Unfortunately, few in the general public realize the link, even those that regularly visit refuges. To reinforce the fact, federal duck stamps are now accepted as a reusable day pass in lieu of an entrance fee at the most heavily used refuges around the country.

The value of duck stamp funds can hardly be underestimated.

Each year in the United States, hundreds of thousands of acres of wetlands — marshes, swamps, bogs, potholes — are drained or otherwise destroyed. As a result, only a tiny fraction of North America's wetlands remain in an undamaged state. Long viewed as wastelands with no redeeming value, they are now recognized as among the most productive ecosystems on earth; an acre of saltmarsh, for example, is far more fertile than even the richest Midwest wheat field. They are the nurseries for a large portion of North America's wildlife, from fish to birds and mammals. Waterfowl, because they are treasured by hunters and birders, get most of the attention, but the refuges protect much, much more.

Typical is the Brigantine unit of the Edwin B. Forsythe National Wildlife Refuge in coastal New Jersey. A dirt road used by visitors follows a circuit for miles out along dikes that separate the tidal marsh from freshwater impoundments. During the winter, tens of thousands of snow geese whiten the tidal flats, feeding on cordgrass. Brant, Canada geese and nearly two dozen species of ducks can be found here during the spring and fall migration, along with thousands of shorebirds, terns, gulls and songbirds. Endangered bald eagles are a common sight here, as are peregrine falcons, which

Neal R. Anderson's lesser scaup pair on the 1989–90 design marked the first time this common diving duck had ever been featured on a federal stamp. New restrictions on subject matter will insure that all forty-two of North America's waterfowl species will eventually be included in the federal series. (© Neal R. Anderson)

were reintroduced to the refuge in the 1970s, after pesticide use largely eliminated them in the East. White-tailed deer, squirrels, muskrats, river otter and red fox live in the refuge's waterways and thickets of holly and pine. In all, more than 32,000 acres are preserved here and at another unit on Long Beach Island, several miles up the coast.

Just across the bay from Brigantine, the casinos and hotels of Atlantic City rise against the horizon. All along this coastline — as across so much of the United States — development pressures are squeezing wildlife into smaller and smaller fragments of habitat. But the National Wildlife Refuges are safe — thanks, in large part, to the legacy of "Ding" Darling's first little stamp.

CHAPTER TWO

The State Programs

© Robert Bateman - 1982

In a way, what is surprising about state duck stamp programs is that it took so long for them to start. The federal program began in 1934, and every year brought in millions of dollars for wetlands preservation; the 1970 design, for example, grossed more than $7 million in stamp sales alone. State wildlife agencies could be forgiven if they envied the federal pot.

In 1971, however, California issued a stamp, becoming the first in a long line of first of state editions — that is, the first stamp and print to be issued by a particular state. The image was a fairly simple drawing by Paul B. Johnson, an artist with the California Department of Fish and Game, and showed a pair of pintails taking off from a reedy marsh.

The stamp was not an immediate success: less than half of the 400,000 that were printed actually sold. But California kept issuing the stamps, which were, like the federal stamp, a form of waterfowl license to be purchased by duck hunters. The next year, 1972, Iowa commissioned native artist Maynard Reece to paint a trio of mallards for its first of state, and in 1974 Maryland and Massachusetts started issuing stamps of their own. By 1976 nine states had stamp programs, and five of them featured open competition to select the paintings that would be used.

Today, more than forty-five states have waterfowl stamps, proving the ultimate success of California's experiment. Even Hawaii — which has no waterfowling tradition and only three native species of ducks and geese — is being pressured to create a stamp, simply to round out the series. While the greatest attention is still focused on the federal program, state stamps, especially first of states, have become a tremendous force in collecting and conservation.

State duck stamps have also seen a remarkable evolution in style. While the artistic quality of the federal program has always been high, many of the early state designs left much to be desired. Part of

Previous page *Amid the leathery fronds of bull kelp, a male harlequin duck bobs on the waves in Robert Bateman's 1988 Washington state design. Bateman, perhaps the most highly regarded wildlife artist in the world, has painted a number of state stamps, as well as the Canadian Wildlife Habitat Conservation Stamp and the inaugural National Fish and Wildlife Foundation Stamp. (© Robert Bateman, courtesy Mill Pond Press)*

A simple drawing of two pintails marked California's 1971 stamp, the first time a state issued a stamp of its own. Since then, more than forty-five other states — not to mention a host of private conservation organizations — have joined in with stamp releases of their own.

*Three Canada geese, members of the
once-threatened "giant" subspecies
native to the Midwest, drift to earth
above a muddy field in Charles W.
Schwartz's 1979 Missouri design.*

A male wigeon flares away in Arthur Eakin's 1981 Maryland design; Eakin had originally painted the work for the federal contest.

The late Ned Smith, considered by many to be one of the deans of American wildlife art, was commissioned by the Pennsylvania Game Commission to paint "Sycamore Creek Woodies" for their first of state in 1983.

the problem was in reproduction. California's first seven stamps, all created by Johnson, were nicely rendered drawings that were then printed in green and brown, often destroying the beauty of the original; the 1976 stamp, a flock of three flying wigeon, was printed with the birds in brown but parts of their wings and heads in green, and the result was an artistic disaster. Even worse was the following year's stamp, in 1978. Lawrence K. Michaelson, (who won the federal contest a year later) won the state's first contest with a colorful painting of two hooded mergansers. But the stamp made from the painting bore only a sophomoric outline drawing of the ducks. Finally, in 1979, California began issuing stamps that reproduced the design in color — something other states had been doing for years.

As the popularity of state stamps grew through the 1970s and early 1980s, the quality of art increased dramatically — partly a result of more sophisticated judging, partly a result of more artists, many of them waterfowl specialists, entering the stamp contests. One of the most outstanding early stamps was the 1975 Maryland design, the state's second. Artist Stanley Stearns, a three-time federal winner, painted a flock of Canada geese flying low over a pine-rimmed lake. Canada geese — this time the giant subspecies of the Midwest — were also depicted on the excellent Missouri first of state by Charles W. Schwartz in 1979; the geese are about to land in a flooded field, their wings back and feet down for the impact.

The 1981 Maryland stamp, by Arthur R. Eakin, is reminiscent of the older school of waterfowl art instead of the modern, photographic look usually favored by duck stamp artists. A single male wigeon, shown flaring away from the viewer against a stormy sky, dominates the work, done in a painterly fashion.

One advantage a state has over the federal duck stamp is the opportunity for a little regional boosterism. Rather than representing the country as a whole, the stamp can include a sense of place — something unique about that state. North Dakota's series has included a painting by Les Kouba of scaup winging past grain elevators, while Maine's first of state by David Maass showed common eiders with the Pemaquid Lighthouse in the foggy distance. Arkansas, among other states, has in recent years made a habit of highlighting actual locales — Bayou DeView in Ken Carlson's 1985 work, Hurricane Lake in Robert Bateman's 1987 work. While not always site-specific, many states, especially those in the West, issue stamps with mountain ranges, or the rocky north Pacific shore, as a backdrop. There is no mistaking such scenes for, say, a New Jersey salt marsh.

With more than forty species of North American waterfowl to choose from, one might expect a great deal of variety in the kinds of birds depicted in stamps; but that isn't the case. There are several reasons for that. Many species of ducks, geese and swans, like the whistling-ducks of the extreme South, have limited ranges; obviously, North Carolina isn't going to print a stamp carrying the likeness of a king eider from the Arctic, nor is landlocked Iowa going to feature a sea duck like the oldsquaw. Furthermore, judges and art committees alike pick birds that are popular with collectors, rather than risk lower print sales by choosing a species that few people are familiar with.

Over the years, the mallard has been the clear favorite, followed (in descending order of frequency) by Canada geese, wood ducks, pintails and canvasbacks; other species consistently popular with painters and judges have been green-winged teal, buffleheads, wigeon, redheads, scaup and snow geese. Others have appeared only once or twice — the common eider on the Maine 1985 stamp, the western black brant on the Oregon 1986 stamp, and the oldsquaw (or at least a decoy of one) on the Massachusetts 1980 stamp. Alaska has concentrated its series on that state's unusual waterfowl — emperor geese for the 1985 first of state, a Stellar's eider in 1986, spectacled eider in 1987, trumpeter swans in 1988 and Barrow's goldeneye in 1989. Washington's 1988 harlequin duck by Robert Bateman was the first time that species had been on a state stamp, although the federal series featured it in the 1950s.

Decoys, Not Ducks

Many state programs, by design or accident, have taken on unique forms. The most striking is Massachusetts', which, since its beginning in 1974, has always featured paintings of decoys by famous carvers. The concept was a Massachusetts first, although it was followed in very short order by James P. Fisher's controversial 1975–6 federal design, showing a canvasback decoy.

The decoys depicted in the Massachusetts designs are not the intricate, decorative carvings seen at modern decoy shows. They are the old working stools of the nineteenth and early twentieth centuries — roughly carved, with minimal attention to detail, but

Sherrie Russell 1988 ©

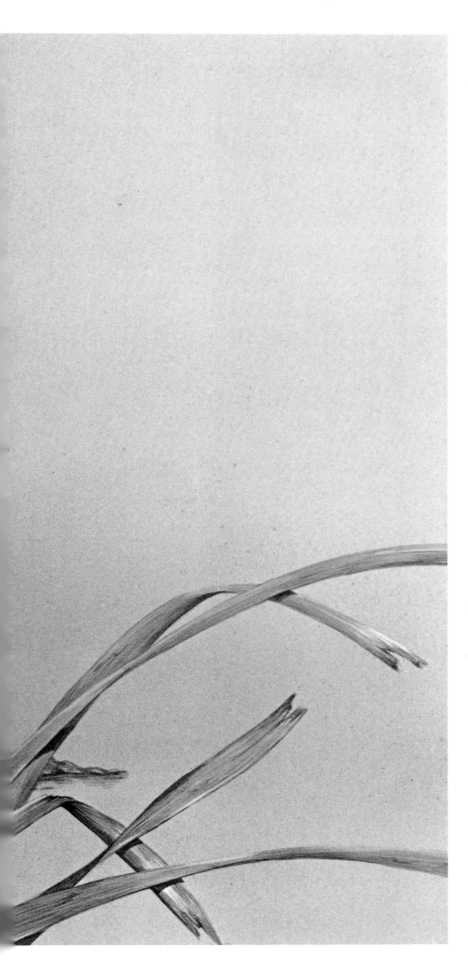

Artist Sherrie Russell chose to show a drake green-winged teal, the smallest of North America's dabbling ducks, sitting quietly on a hummock in the 1988 Arizona stamp and print. Like many states, the size of the Arizona print edition is based on the number of orders received by a set date; in other states, the edition size is predetermined.

1985 Alaska Waterfowl Stamp

1987 Alaska Waterfowl Stamp

*Trumpeter swans fly beneath Alaska's
verdant coastal mountains in that
state's 1988 stamp, designed by artist
James Beaudion (top). The 1985 first
of state by Daniel Smith, shows*

*emperor geese (left), and the 1987 by
Carl Branson is a painting of two
spectacled eiders (right). Alaska has
made a practice of highlighting its
unique arctic species.*

with an artistic flair that belies their crude beginnings. The third Massachusetts stamp, from 1976, shows a floating Canada goose decoy, head arching down to the water in a graceful curve, its lead keel still in place. The 1980 design, a slat-and-canvas oldsquaw, shows the worn paint and scuffed wooden head of the original, the product of hard use on the open ocean where these sea-going ducks are hunted.

Massachusetts' decoy-oriented program is unique in another way — it is the only "duck" stamp series to routinely include species other than waterfowl. In 1979, artist Randy Julius won the contest with a painting of a classic ruddy turnstone decoy, a feat repeated in 1982 by John Eggert with a design showing a greater yellowlegs decoy. Both the turnstone and yellowlegs are shorebirds, and in the nineteenth century — when the decoys themselves were carved — they were hunted for market along with ducks and geese.

Decoys have shown up occasionally on other state stamps, although many programs insist that living waterfowl must be the focus of a winning entry. Nevada's first of state design in 1979 was a dramatic composition by Larry Hayden of an ancient Indian reed decoy, fashioned with feathers into an elegant imitation of a

Rather than sponsoring an open contest, Arkansas commissions well-known artists, who are asked to feature actual locations in their paintings. This is David Maass' "Black River Green-winged Teal," 1983.

Another state that uses its natural beauty to advantage in its duck stamps is Vermont; "Winter Goldeneyes" by artist Jim Killen shows three common goldeneyes flying over Lake Champlain. (© State of Vermont)

One of the most unusual state stamp series is that of Massachusetts, which each year features a painting of an actual classic decoy. And as is shown by the 1979 stamp, which carries the image of a ruddy turnstone decoy, Massachusetts is the only state to regularly use birds other than ducks, geese or swans.

Sidelighting and a warm violet wash convey the feeling of sundown in Brian Jarvi's 1986 Minnesota design, showing a pair of lesser scaup.

canvasback; the painting also included a pair of canvasbacks flying against a stylized sun, and Indian pottery designs.

The 1984 California design, by artist Robert Montanucci, was a simple still-life of a mallard decoy, a duck call and two shotgun shells, while the 1980 Maryland design took the whole decoy aspect a step further, by featuring Lem and Steve Ward, the premier decoy carvers of the Eastern Shore. With the small portrait of the brothers was a painting of one of their pintail dekes, and a vignette showing the decoy's underside, with their signature. Jack Schroeder, himself an Eastern Shore artist, designed the stamp.

Editions, Commissions and Contests

An art buyer entering the duck stamp market will find a wide variety of products available. The stamp itself, of course, is the foundation, and is universally the cheapest item, usually costing less than $10. Prints are issued in limited editions — that is, the number of prints made is restricted, either set ahead of time or determined by how many are sold within a certain period (a "time-limited" edition).

Four wood ducks fly in loose formation over a beaver pond in the 1987 New York design by Lee LeBlanc. The loosely rendered painting shows the species in a typical setting in the Northeast, where it is one of the most common ducks, among the crisp colors of autumn.

Limited editions are signed in the margin by the artist, and numbered sequentially, showing the edition size and the individual print's place in the run; the first print of a 900-print edition, for instance, is numbered 1/900, the last, 900/900. Many print aficionados collect only the same numbers from each edition, and can reserve their number for future prints.

Also predetermined is the number of artist's proofs, generally 50 or 100, that are made above and beyond the edition size. Artist's proofs were originally extra prints made so the artist could check the fidelity of the reproduction, but today they are viewed as part of the compensation package, available to the artist for resale or donation.

How the art is selected varies from state to state. In more than two-thirds, it is chosen as a result of contests, usually open to anyone regardless of residence, although eight states restrict their contests to state residents only. Pennsylvania, which began its program in 1983 with a commissioned painting by the late Ned Smith, switched to competition in 1986. For the next three years the contest was open to any artist, regardless of residence, and was consistently won by out-of-staters. Starting in 1989, entries were limited to Pennsylvania artists only, primarily to promote print sales within the state itself.

A male greater scaup rears back to flap his wings as the rest of the flock rides the heavy swells of Lake Ontario in Robert Bateman's 1989 New York design. Sales of Bateman's duck stamps and prints have been consistently high, making him a much sought-after artist for stamp programs. (Above) The 1989 New York stamp, which is not required for waterfowl hunters. (© Robert Bateman, courtesy Mill Pond Press)

In the other eleven states that have duck stamp programs, the art is chosen by commission, often in cooperation with a print publisher, state waterfowl committee or state Ducks Unlimited chapter, which may share in the proceeds. While contests provide struggling artists with an opening to the rarefied world of duck stamps, commissions usually go to respected artists with proven sales records, whose prints and stamps are sure to outsell a relatively unknown new-comer.

New York has commissioned each of its waterfowl stamp designs since the program's inception in 1985. Nancy Schneider, fish and wildlife marketing specialist for that state's Department of Environmental Conservation, said the commission process gives the state a greater role in what the image will include.

"If you look at New York's artwork, it's a little bit different than some of the other states in that it doesn't usually focus on a species in a real close-up situation, sitting on the water — we've strayed from that, and purposely. Some of the things we wanted to do were represent habitat indicative of New York, species indicative of New York, and the hand of man in each one of these images. Beginning in 1985 with Larry Barton's Canada goose flock it was a duck blind, and we have had a beaver dam with wood duck boxes in 1987, and pintails coming across a farmer's fields in the shadow of a barn in 1988." True to form, the 1989 painting, by Robert Bateman, shows a flock of greater scaup with a commercial fishing boat on the horizon.

"We've also tried to focus a lot on the habitat, maybe equal to the species," Schneider said. "A lot of times artists place an emphasis on one or the other, and we've struggled to have an equal representation of those two elements, if possible."

Commissioning Bateman was a sound decision for New York from several perspectives. By law, half of the money the state raises from sales of its stamps and prints must be spent on waterfowl conservation in Canada; Bateman is a Canadian with a very strong following in his native country, which could only help boost New York's cross-border sales. His art is wildly popular in the United States as well, so a strong United States market could be expected. And also important, Schneider said, is the fact that Mill Pond Press, Bateman's publisher, has a strong marketing structure in Canada, which would leave the state positioned well there in the years ahead.

Breaking With Conformity

Robert Bateman, the Canadian artist who has set the wildlife art world on its ear in the past ten years (and who has disparaged most duck stamp painting as "cookie-cutter art") has created a number of commissioned works for states, the National Fish and Wildlife Foundation and for the Canadian Wildlife Habitat Conservation series. As might be expected of an artist who broke many of the constraints that had hobbled animal art for years, Bateman's duck stamp paintings have a delightful freshness of approach.

In a genre that usually demands artificially brilliant colors and bright, almost harsh lighting, Bateman's paintings have a feeling of subdued atmospherics. "Rolling Waves," his painting of greater scaup for New York's 1989 stamp and print, is only a step away from monochromatic; the heavy swells of Lake Ontario reflect the gray clouds overhead, and match the steely plumage of the rafting ducks. The only touches of color are the greenish heads of the drakes, and the brown bodies of the hens. Schneider said that when the finished painting was shown to biologists (who check each year's image for accuracy), they quickly noticed a playful touch Bateman had slipped in — a male common goldeneye floating among the raft of scaup.

Likewise, Bateman's 1988 Washington design, a male harlequin duck among floating fronds of bull kelp, shows the same disregard for the usual conventions of duck stamp art. It features one of the lesser-known species of North American waterfowl, a bird whose bizarre color pattern would be garish if handled with less sensitivity.

Not every artist is able to play so fast and loose with the unwritten rules of stamp art. Artists entering open competition might like to paint an unusual pose, use dramatic lighting or show a unique behavior, but most realize that their chances are better if they stick to the proven formula: a pair (or small flock) in full breeding plumage, with the drake pre-eminent in the composition and a simple background — misty vignettes or a distant line of reeds are

*Robert Steiner's pair of cinnamon teal
(above) beat a wide field to capture the
1989 California contest; the other
finalists (opposite, clockwise from top
right) were Susan Bates, Vicki
Hummel, Sherrie Russell, and Roger
Cruwys.*

Pemaquid Lighthouse, which guards
the rocky shore near New Harbor,
Maine, was the setting for David
Maass' 1985 Maine stamp, which
shows three common eiders in flight.
(Right) The 1988 Maine stamp.

1988 MAINE MIGRATORY WATERFOWL STAMP

standard — with the birds flatteringly lit. The result, as Bateman's critical remark suggests, is often a stultifying lack of variety, and many stamp designs are so clichéd as to be virtually interchangeable.

"The problem is in the judging," claims Virginia artist Ron Louque. "A great painting does not always win these things. Bad paintings can win them — you'll have fantastic art right up next to them (that doesn't win), and it's frustrating. The art is getting better, but the judges are not always on the same level as the artists." In consequence, he thinks, judges tend to pick overworked designs instead of those showing a fresh approach.

Robert Steiner, who has set a record for designing more state stamps than anyone else, thinks part of the trouble is artists who try too hard to out-think judges.

"I do a lot of thinking about the design and what the judges might be looking for, and in the past I may have done more thinking than I do now. After a while you realize there's no way to think it out. A lot of artists, especially when they're first starting to compete, try to figure the whole thing out, try to figure out exactly what the judges might be looking for. But . . . the judges aren't looking for anything — they're sitting there looking at what you have to show them, just

Daniel Smith's acrylic of a pair of wood ducks in a cypress swamp beat more than thirty-five competitors to become Georgia's first of state duck stamp design in 1985. The painting shows the meticulous rendering that brought Smith the top spot in the 1988–89 federal contest, as well as a number of state programs.

65

Ralph J. McDonald's whimsical painting of a retriever pup and a mallard duckling, painted for the 1989 Georgia stamp, is representative of the unusual approaches many artists, and states, are now taking.

Harold Roe's 1987 Ohio design shows a great deal of depth in its approach to a pair of blue-winged teal and their habitat. The artist chose a tricky, foreshortened view of the drake's head, and managed to keep the intricate background of dead limbs and reeds from detracting from the main subjects.

looking for the best piece. If it's exactly like last year's, I don't think it's really going to bother them. A lot of them might not even be aware of what last year's was — but a lot of artists are *highly* aware. They're basing a lot of their thinking on that, when the judges might not be basing nearly as much," Steiner said.

A Fresh Approach

Happily, many of the states (and judges) appear to recognize the repetition in duck stamps, and in recent years there has been a refreshing break from the formulaic designs of the past. West Virginia, for example, is making a conscious effort to choose stamps with an unusual approach; for the 1989 design, Louque was commissioned to paint a still-life of decoys in a barn, while the 1988 painting by South Carolina artist Steve Dillard featured a female wood duck with her chicks — but without her gorgeously colored mate — chosen in open competition.

According to Charles M. Heartwell III, a cold-water fisheries

"Hurricane Lake — Wood Ducks" by Robert Bateman is another in the Arkansas series, this from 1987. Typical of Bateman's pronounced atmospherics and well-thought composition, the painting takes a colorful subject — wood duck drakes — and mutes their brilliance as nature would on an overcast day. (© Robert Bateman, courtesy Mill Pond Press)

67

After their publisher backed out of a deal, New Hampshire's Fish and Game Department scrambled to arrange for printing and distribution of Durant Ball's 1986 design. The result was a "Made in New Hampshire" edition that won a number of prestigious printing awards.

*Colorful fall foliage partially obscures
a trio of wood ducks by Thomas Gross,
the artist for this 1984 Minnesota
design. (Above) Three other
Minnesota stamps — canvasbacks by
James Meger; common goldeneyes by
Ron Van Gilder; and wigeon by Jim
Hautman.*

69

biologist who does double-duty for the West Virginia Department of Natural Resources by running its duck stamp program, a lot of thought goes into selecting an artist and a theme for a new painting.

"When we got into the duck stamp business, it became painfully obvious that there were 5,000 pieces of average art out there, most of which depict two ducks flying or two ducks sitting, with no attempt to make a message. We thought that since we're going to be in this business, we'd like to try to make a conservation statement," he said.

"The 1988 image equated the comeback of the wood duck to what we hope to do with waterfowl populations in general in West Virginia working with the stamp and print money," Heartwell said. "Just as the wood duck was brought back to relative abundance through conservation, we hope through the expenditure of this money to bring other ducks back. The 1989 design was a thank-you to the co-authors and co-sponsors of the North American Waterfowl Management Plan (an ambitious public-private undertaking to stabilize declining duck populations), with a special thank-you to Ducks Unlimited, which is the strongest private conservation group in duck management."

Redheads were the subject for Indiana's 1988 stamp and print, painted by Bruce Langton. Many duck stamp artists have particular species that they prefer to paint; Langton had won the Delaware contest the year before with another painting of swimming redheads.

The selection of artist Ron Louque was the result of just as much forethought. "Ron was someone up-and-coming who had recognition, who had done five state programs, who's well thought-of personally, whose art is well thought-of and is improving all the time." Louque had also just done the first of state edition for neighboring Virginia, so West Virginia officials thought they could benefit from the major advertising campaign Virginia had run. "We put all those things together, and we went after the man we wanted to do it," Heartwell said.

Louque and West Virginia officials discussed the theme. The state wanted the art to feature mallards, pintails and black ducks, the three species that the North American Waterfowl Management Plan focuses on. But ducks of different species rarely mingle in the wild, so they decided to use decoys.

"We started out with a decoy carver painting some decoys in a shop, but the artist didn't like that — he thought it was too 'new'." Instead, Louque suggested something more historical — a still-life of actual decoys from actual carvers. Heartwell at first wanted to feature the work of the famous Ward brothers of Maryland's Eastern Shore,

A hen wood duck with her brood, the 1988 West Virginia design, was meant to be more than an attractive painting. The work, by artist Steve Dillard, was intended to symbolize the resurgence of the once-rare woodie, and by implication, the conservation of waterfowl in general.

A pair of canvasbacks rests quietly on the waves in Tom Hirata's 1985 North Carolina stamp and print. This species and this setting was a lucky combination for Hirata, who used it in a similar painting for New Jersey in 1984.

but settled instead for the decoys of R. Madison Mitchell, a Havre de Grace, Maryland, carver who's works are still available. "We felt as long as we were going to use decoys, we'd give a contemporary carver a plug," Heartwell said.

The finished painting shows four decoys, freshly repainted for the upcoming duck season, drying on an old apple crate. In the straw nearby is a copy of the 50th anniversary issue of *Ducks Unlimited*.

The inclusion of the magazine was more than just a casual tip of the hat toward the conservation group. Using it as a selling point, Heartwell then convinced Ducks Unlimited to purchase 2,000 prints and stamps, to be sold in a national campaign, which is something the group rarely does for state designs. The unique image (one of very few still-life stamps ever done) also brought tiny West Virginia into a partnership with Alaska, Louisiana and Oklahoma to jointly issue governor's editions, signed by the heads of each state.

"We're a poor state from a waterfowl perspective," Heartwell said. "We're a landlocked state, not in a strong migratory pattern, and we do not have a lot of discretionary income, so it's very difficult to keep a waterfowl program here in the black. Anything we can do to make money for our program, we really appreciate."

Prints for the Wall, Money for the Ducks

While many print and stamp buyers are keenly aware of the conservation value inherent in duck stamps, most collect them for their artistic merit. That does not make the financial windfall any less important for state wildlife agencies, however, as they face the prospect of ever-shrinking wetlands for waterfowl and other wildlife.

Alaska, which issued its first of state stamp and print in 1985, has raised more than $1.6 million for its wetlands conservation projects. The money has been spent, according to Thomas C. Rothe, state waterfowl coordinator, on the establishment of a population of the Vancouver subspecies of Canada geese on Kodiak Island; creation of roosting and feeding areas for sandhill cranes in Fairbanks to lure them away from the city airport; purchases of large tracts of land for waterfowl and other wetlands inhabitants, and the enhancement of existing refuges. At the Palmer Hay Flats State Game Refuge, for example, the state worked with Ducks Unlimited to create thirteen ponds and nesting islands, three miles of connecting channels, and test revegetation techniques for use in coastal regions. A similar project on a smaller scale was carried out at a waterfowl refuge near Fairbanks, and the state has even used stamp funds to seek solutions to the burgeoning population of mallards in Anchorage.

Pennsylvania, which earns about $125,000 to $150,000 a year from sales of stamps and prints, has used some of its money to purchase large tracts of wetlands along the Allegheny River for use as new state game lands, open to hunting, bird-watching and hiking. Using duck stamp funds in conjunction with Duck Unlimited's MARSH (Matching Aid to Restore State Habitats) program, the state bought a "cookie-cutter," a machine that cuts clear swaths through choking marsh vegetation, creating channels and openings for waterfowl.

Late day sun models the form of two pintails in Larry Barton's 1987 North Carolina design. As with most duck stamp art, the painting carefully shows off the most attractive points of its subjects — the drake's brown and white head, his long tail feathers, and the iridescent speculum on the secondary wing feathers.

73

With a distinctly Southern skyline of palmettos behind them, two canvasbacks zoom in for splashdown in the 1986 Florida stamp and print by Robert Steiner.

*Maynard Reece, who has won so many
duck stamp competitions in his long
career, now designs stamps only on
commission. Such was the case with
"Big Lake Wood Ducks," his 1982
Arkansas painting.*

75

A dentist who enjoys art in his free time, Richard L. Wilson painted the winning entry for the 1985 California stamp contest, depicting a pair of ring-necked ducks.

New York's program is unique in that half the duck stamp money the state raises must be spent on waterfowl projects in Canada. There is clear biological thinking behind the decision; the majority of North America's ducks, geese and swans breed in Canada but winter in the United States, making their conservation an international concern. Rockland Marsh in New Brunswick, for example, is a profoundly fertile salt marsh with the potential to be even more important for black ducks. One of the first joint New York-Canadian projects took place there; dikes were built to stabilize water levels, creating perfect conditions for the invertebrates that ducklings need to feed on in their first weeks. Nesting islands, which offer protection from predators, and mowed channels in dense cattail stands were also made.

A second joint project took place at Balmoral Marsh in Ontario, on the shores of Lake St. Clair, one of the most important waterfowl staging areas in eastern Canada. Privately owned, the 178 acre marsh was in danger of being drained, but thanks in part to New York duck stamp money, a long-term agreement with the landowner was reached, and the failing dikes and poor water supply repaired.

West Virginia also allocates half of its funds for Canadian work, and tries, as much as possible, to find matching funds for wetlands conservation within the state's boundaries. "So far," Heartwell said, "we have been able to at least match all the waterfowl money we are spending, and because of two or three other federal deals we have been able to triple and quadruple it in some cases." The money has not been idle, despite deep-seated opposition in some quarters to the idea of preserving what is seen as wasteland.

"Swamps are not popular in West Virginia — agriculture is, where you have flatlands," Heartwell explained. "We have purchased some extremely valuable habitat here which would have been lost otherwise. We've secured long-term purchase rights on other parcels, and we have a statewide waterfowl marsh management plan whereby if any piece of habitat is imminently threatened, this money allows us to go snatch it up or get some kind of agreement on it right away."

In New Hampshire, duck stamp funds have gone toward the purchase of marshes, bogs and other imperiled wetlands, as well as allowing the state Fish and Game Department to provide professional biologists to work with the New Hampshire Waterfowl Association

The Rev. Samuel Timm, a Wisconsin minister who painted a pair of hooded mergansers for the 1988 Wisconsin stamp, has captured a number of other conservation stamp and wildlife art honors.

Using a buoyant watercolor technique, artist Jim Killen captures the vitality of mallards on the wing in the 1986 Georgia design, which he was commissioned to paint. Georgia has used its stamp funds to purchase land, erect wood duck boxes and maintain a growing resident population of Canada geese.

and Ducks Unlimited on private conservation projects. The state is also erecting nest boxes for wood ducks (one of the most important waterfowl species in the East) and employing moist soil management techniques on its land to ensure the perfect stage of aquatic plant growth for ducks.

CHAPTER THREE

The Artists

©88 Chris White

Christopher White, a 30-year-old illustrator who works at the military's Aberdeen Proving Grounds in Maryland, was out of his office one day in March 1988 when a telephone call came for him from the coordinator of Maryland's duck stamp contest. When White got back to his desk and received the message, the news set off butterflies in his stomach.

Several weeks before, he had finished an acrylic painting of two ruddy ducks, which he submitted for the Maryland waterfowl stamp contest. As White well knew, this was the day of the judging.

"On the one hand I was frantic, thinking 'My God, is that what it is, is that what it is?' Then on the other hand, it was 'Now wait, don't get your hopes up, maybe it was just something like all the paintings were lost in a fire.' " For an hour and a half, White swung from one extreme to another. "It was pins and needles — I got no work done," he said.

Finally, the coordinator called back with the news that his painting, "Early Spring Ruddies," had beaten 124 other works to win the state's fifteenth duck stamp contest.

"When she called, I literally almost fainted," White said. "My knees went weak and I just kind of fell down in the chair."

Previous page "Early Spring Ruddies," *by Christopher White, was the result of field work, reference photographs and research. It won the 1988 Maryland contest, an event that dramatically changed White's life.*

Green-winged teal pitch headlong to the water, with rugged, snow-capped peaks in the background. The image was painted by Jim Killen for the 1988–89 Idaho stamp and print.

*Arizona kicked off its waterfowl stamp
program in 1987 with this first of state
by Daniel Smith, showing a pair of
pintails. (Above) Two of Ohio's
stamps — the 1986 by Lynn Kaatz,
and the 1983 by Harry Antis.*

For many relatively unknown artists like White, the telephone call announcing the selection of their painting as a duck stamp may mean the beginning of a whole new life, and the fulfillment of long-held dreams. In one fell swoop, national attention, name recognition, substantial financial gains — all the things struggling artists hope for — may be there for the taking. Duck stamps have launched or cemented the careers of many respected wildlife artists: David Maass, Maynard Reece, Edward Bierly, Al Gilbert, Richard Plasschaert, Dan Smith, Robert Steiner and others.

The key to getting the most financially from a duck stamp win is in limited edition print sales. Some states market prints themselves, or through a contractor, and pay the winning artist a cut (Pennsylvania, for example, has an agreement with a state publisher, who handles sales and pays the artist $3 for each $140.50 print sold). In neighboring Maryland, where White won, the state uses the painting to create the stamp, but returns all rights to the artist.

"It's up to the artist to produce the print, market, distribute," White said. "You can either go with an outside publisher — I had two approach me — but I decided to do the whole thing myself. And while it's a lot of work, and I've learned a whole lot about publishing

Guy Coheleach, who enjoys international notoriety for his stylistically variable wildlife art, created his first duck stamp in 1987 for the Kansas first of state; the subjects are green-winged teal.

Canada geese have always been
popular duck stamp subjects. Ann C.
Dohoney painted a pair for the 1988
Kansas stamp, while the species was
featured on two of the early federal
series. (Opposite) Three geese come in
for a landing in the 1936–37 federal by
Richard E. Bishop. (Overleaf) For the
1958–59 stamp, Les Kouba depicted a
flock joining birds already feeding in a
cornfield.

Duck Stamp Design - 1936

and limited edition prints and dealers and galleries and all, the profit goes to the artist." White's wife Jan took a year off from her teaching job to handle the bookwork and shipping, and the Aberdeen Proving Grounds granted White three days a week off without pay to do the signing, numbering and remarquing that a print edition requires. It is an onerous load of work, and most successful stamp artists end up actually painting less than they did before the win.

Artistic Heritage

Every artist who paints a duck stamp comes to the genre with a different artistic vision, bringing different backgrounds and skills. Some are illustrators, others classically trained in the fine arts. Many are self-taught, drawn at first more by a love of the outdoors, and of birds, than a passion for art itself.

For Ron Louque, a native of Louisiana, the path led from the bayous to college zoology classes — all with no idea of ever pursuing art, even as a hobby.

"I never planned on being an artist, never. I was involved in

taxidermy as a child, and living in Louisiana I hunted and fished all the time," he said. "I was kind of a unique kid — my life centered around collecting a variety of specimens, taking the things home and mounting them. By the time I was a senior in high school, I must have had 300 or 400 birds stuffed in every closet, and on every shelf and chest of drawers.

"When I went to college (at Louisiana State University), my intention was actually to be a wildlife biologist. I must have been in my second year when I ran into a museum preparator who was doing dioramas, habitat groups. I really got swayed by that."

Art had made its first bow into Ron Louque's life.

At roughly the same time, Louque met two graduate students at the university who were to be important influences on his life. Doug Pratt and John P. O'Neill, both of whom have gone on to establish reputations for their bird art, introduced Louque to painting. It was a revelation.

"That was my first dose of art, right there. Had I been introduced to it earlier perhaps I would have been interested in it, but I grew up in the sticks, and I don't think I'd seen a painting until that time. But I immediately took to it. It seemed to go pretty well for me — I had a

A self-taught artist and accomplished field naturalist, Ned Smith's paintings, like the 1985 Pennsylvania design shown here, had absolute fidelity to the correct habitat, and almost total accuracy to the subject.

(Overleaf) A shaft of sunlight catches decoys being prepared for the upcoming season in Ron Louque's painting, used to create the 1989 West Virginia stamp and print. The decoys represent mallards, black ducks and pintails, the three species that the North American Waterfowl Management Plan seeks to help, while the rumpled copy of Ducks Unlimited *magazine is meant as a salute to that organization.*

89

Ronald J. Louque

good background in wildlife and birds, nature habitat." And taxidermy. "Oh yes," Louque laughed, "taking them apart and putting them back together again." Louque had switched from wildlife management to the zoology program, losing about fifteen hours of credit because of the move. He was so caught up with the idea of painting that he didn't make up the lost time, but jumped right into art as a career.

"I decided I wanted to paint, and that was it. I said it's now or never — I was so taken with it I really couldn't concentrate on my studies," he recalled. A decision that takes many artists years to reach came for Louque after only two years of painting. "I did it quite prematurely, because I really knew very little about art ... I was so ignorant — looking back, it was a plain miracle that I made it."

Actually, Louque's illustrative technique and scientific background were tailor-made for duck stamps. He started entering the federal competition in 1973, but his first win didn't come until 1985, when he captured the Ohio contest. Since then, the wins and the commissions have come with increasing regularity. Yet, just as Louque's style is bringing him notoriety, he finds himself (as have so many artists before him) drawn increasingly to looser, more artistically rendered works, instead of the tight style demanded by contest judges.

"I'm beginning to learn what art is now. I was making — well, I thought it was art, and I guess it's a kind of art, but I was mainly just illustrating birds," he said.

Christopher White makes no apologies for being an illustrator — it is something he does for a living. "I wish I could give you some lofty ideas of mine, and say 'Yes, my goal in art is to open the eyes of the world to some new movement,' but realistically I'm an illustrator," White said. "When I grew up it was illustrators whose work I admired. I like the idea of someone referring to a book or a story or a magazine, then looking at my artwork and saying, 'Boy, he hit that idea right on the head.' " He brings that sense of creating a scene to his art. "Early Spring Ruddies," his winning Maryland painting, uses a few wild plum blossoms, fallen from the trees and floating beside the pair of ducks, to create a feeling of time and place — spring on a tributary of the Chesapeake Bay, where plum trees overhang the banks, dropping their flowers like snow.

Of course, no painting appears magically on the board. White invested weeks of planning and research in his work. Fresh from winning the state's trout stamp contest, he had set his sights on the duck stamp as his next goal, and he was determined to do as much as he could to improve his chances.

"My intention was to do a small species, and I had decided on either buffleheads or ruddy ducks. There's just something about the small, compact round bodies that I wanted to paint — no other reason, but I didn't know which one to do. I was out watching waterfowl on the Bay, and I saw some ruddies there — too far to get any good reference photos, but just watching the two of them, a male and female, interact was captivating."

With his decision made, White set about getting reference material. He called zoos in the region, and discovered that the National Zoo in Washington D.C. had ruddy ducks in its aviary collection. On two weekends he drove down to the zoo, shooting roll after roll of slides.

Evolution of a Duck Stamp

California artist Robert Steiner rejected two designs for his Rhode Island 1989 painting before settling on the final concept, showing a pair of canvasbacks against the backdrop of Pettaquamscutt Cove in that state. The final drawing (below) was transferred to a Masonite board prepared with toned gesso, then Steiner did a complete underpainting in burnt sienna before moving to color.

*White-caps boil beneath three lesser
scaup, in the 1977 Iowa duck stamp,
painted in oils by Maynard Reece.*

He also dug out every book he could find about ruddies, learning all he could about this odd species of duck.

"I started working on the sketches, working from the photographs. I figured if I was entering a competition in which the judges are sticklers for detail, and everything has to be correct, then that was the safest way to do it. I had about six or seven thumbnail sketches, and the one that I chose, with the male in the background and the female toward the front, is from two different photos. . . . That little bit of motion from the upper right towards the lower left I definitely wanted to have, that little bit of forward motion."

White, like the majority of duck stamp artists, uses acrylics for his work. "You can work it as a watercolor, you can work it as an oil. The water in the painting is painted mostly opaque — the ducks as well, but you'll find certain areas where I put down whites or a lighter color and laid on washes to get a nice tonal value, like the male's plumage."

Creating Within Limits

An artist entering a contest works within a number of firm guidelines. The size of the painting is set, although this varies from contest to contest; for years the federal competition required a tiny 5-by-7-inch format (since changed to 8-by-10-inch), while some of the state guidelines call for paintings as large as 13-by-18 inches. Some contests allow pencil or ink work, while others are restricted to colored media.

Increasingly, the species that can be depicted is being orchestrated as well. Many states declare as ineligible the species selected the previous one, three or five years, to avoid duplicating themselves. The federal duck stamp office now announces, prior to opening the contest each year, a field of five species that will be considered — a move spurred by the realization that in more than 50 years of federal duck stamps, several types of waterfowl have never been featured. A few states will even pick a single species as the subject of that year's competition, putting all the artists on a more even footing.

A commissioned painting can restrict the artist even further, although a fertile imagination can find a myriad of ways to work even within the commission's guidelines. Louque, who was commissioned to do the 1989 West Virginia stamp, was told that the painting should highlight the North American Waterfowl Management Plan and the role that Ducks Unlimited has played in conservation. Furthermore, he was told, the art should have three species of ducks — mallard, pintail and black — a mix rarely found in nature.

Tundra swans (then known as whistling swans) fly against a wooded backdrop in the 1966–67 federal design by Maryland artist Stanley Stearns. Stearns won the federal contest three times, a record only exceeded by Maynard Reece, with five wins, and matched by Edward Bierly.

95

The Reece Family: A Duck Stamp Dynasty

Between them, Maynard Reece and his two sons have designed more than a dozen state and federal duck stamps. (Above) Maynard Reece's 1971–72 federal, only the second to be produced in color. (Right) Mark Reece's 1975 Iowa; (Opposite, top) Brad Reece's 1981 Iowa; and (bottom) Maynard Reece's first duck stamp, the 1948–49 federal design.

96

At first, he and West Virginia officials considered doing an old decoy-carver's shop, but Louque quickly discarded the notion.

"I didn't have much experience with the shops, plus it would have made a cluttered piece, especially for a duck stamp, which has to be fairly simple to begin with," Louque said. "So I put it in a more natural setting, where a hunter had been out in the decoy shed fixing up his decoys before the start of the season — he left the knife sitting on an old apple crate, the string, the old decoy weight and paint can. You could tell he'd just been there. Then the old *Ducks Unlimited* magazine on the floor, kind of like it had been just thrown down there, as if he might have stopped for a break with the magazine."

The decoys were a mix of the three species West Virginia wanted. The message was subtle, but Louque's artistry had fulfilled all the preconditions, while still producing a very pleasing image.

To many people, that's all most duck stamps are — pleasing images; the term "fine art" is rarely applied to them. The stigma of illustration is one that wildlife art in general suffers under, with much justification, it must be said, because so much wildlife painting, especially duck stamps, is formulaic. But the blanket

Balanced composition, detailed backgrounds and plenty of action have helped to make Robert Steiner the winningest duck stamp artist in history. This is his 1987 New Hampshire painting, an acrylic of two Canada geese.

*Calm pervades Tom Hirata's 1987
Tennessee design (top), with only a
ripple to disturb the serenity. Leon
Parson chose vigorous action for his
1986 first of state Utah painting (left),
showing tundra swans in flight over a
valley marsh.*

Stillwater National Wildlife Refuge,
which protects a remnant of Nevada's
once-great Stillwater Marsh, is the
setting for Robert Steiner's 1984
Nevada design.

Jim Lamb's painting of two canvasback drakes was selected for the 1988 Tennessee stamp and print. Unlike many states, which dedicate stamp funds only for waterfowl, Tennessee uses stamp money for general wildlife work.

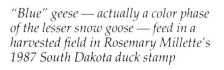

"Blue" geese — actually a color phase of the lesser snow goose — feed in a harvested field in Rosemary Millette's 1987 South Dakota duck stamp design. (Bottom) Two other South Dakota stamps — the 1976 first of state by Robert Kusserow, and the 1986 by John Wilson.

condemnation, often even voiced by other animal artists, irks many of the top stamp artists, who see themselves challenging finely drawn limits and making good art at the same time.

San Francisco artist Robert Steiner, who has won a record twelve state contests, bristled when asked about critics' comments disparaging duck stamp art as cliched, but quickly relaxed.

"They have a point — it's a field in which the parameters are clearly defined, and that's not very common in art. Wildlife art in general has more defined parameters than most art, and I think that's one reason people love it . . . I really like the limitations of duck stamp art. I decided that a lot of great art is produced when the parameters are very narrow, so it requires creativity. Originality for its own sake is pointless. In duck stamps, there are definite limits to how original you can be, yet I find that highly challenging, to come up with something new in such tight restrictions."

Maynard Reece, who has won the prestigious federal contest five times (more than anyone else) voices the same opinion. "Duck stamp art is a very specialized market, and people who work in it must do specialized designs. Because it must be a tiny size the impact must be strong — it can't be a muted, subtle thing," he said. "I wouldn't call one art and the other non-art, because as far as I'm concerned it's all art, just different types. Whether or not one chooses to call it fine art or illustration, to me it's just muddling up a confusion anyhow."

Reece does have misgivings about the trend in modern duck stamp art, however. "Rather than too specialized, I think it's becoming too repetitious. They've concentrated so much on the impact — the larger the bird is, the more impact — that they're ending up with nothing but sitting birds on the water; they can make them bigger that way because the wings aren't outstretched. It has limited the versatility of the design, and I think that's wrong. They should go back to worrying more about the overall composition and whether it depicts the species naturally, whether it gives a pleasing effect and reproduces well."

Reece's name, perhaps more than any other except founder "Ding" Darling's, is associated with the federal duck stamp program. Despite that, although Reece feels his five wins have aided his painting career, he doesn't put most of the credit on duck stamps. "It's been helpful, I'm sure, but it's probably not been the underlying factor that it has with so many of the younger artists. Most of the federal stamps were done before it had such notoriety. . . . But it certainly has been helpful to spread my name around."

Indeed it has; Reece is one of the best-known of American wildlife artists. These days, he divides his time between homes in Florida and Iowa, and only paints duck stamps by commission — the 1988 Arkansas design, the 1989 Washington stamp, and the 1988 print and stamp for the National Fish and Wildlife Foundation, for example. The Foundation's painting was a trademark Reece — two mallards dropping down into reeds, against a gray sky that any waterfowler would recognize instantly.

As Reece's two sons, Mark and Brad, were growing up, they were understandably immersed in their father's art and his love of the outdoors. They eventually followed him, at least briefly, into duck stamp art as well. In 1975, Mark Reece won the Iowa state contest,

Four of Minnesota's stamps: (from top) the 1977 first of state by David Maass; the 1982 redheads by Phil Scholer; 1983 snow and "blue" geese by Gary Moss; and 1988 buffleheads by Robert Hautman.

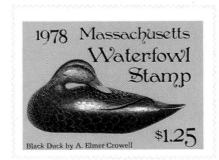

besting 100 other entries with his painting of a flying pair of Canada geese. Six years later, Brad Reece also won the Iowa competition in an equally stiff field; his painting depicts green-winged teal over a sun-lit marsh. Both brothers' work, not surprisingly, shows a strong family resemblance to their father's, especially in color handling and composition. Unlike many young artists who view a duck stamp win as a major step in an art career, both of the young Reeces later gave up wildlife art as a profession — Mark became a plastic surgeon, and Brad opened the Maynard Reece Gallery in Des Moines.

Robert Steiner: King of the Hill

With twelve state designs to his credit, San Francisco artist Robert Steiner has eclipsed all his competitors at the art and business of winning duck stamp contests. His record is enviable in this highly competitive field — in 1989, for instance, he won all four of the contests or bidding fields he entered.

An East Coast native, Steiner brings a solid background in classical art techniques and design to his duck stamp work. He came rather late to strict wildlife painting — until 1979, he was doing what he describes as "kind of philosophical, surrealistic pieces with animals and people put together," as well as landscapes and abstract works. A freelance magazine illustrator and college instructor at the time, Steiner was intrigued by an article on the popularity of duck stamp prints, since he was then heavily involved in creating etchings and lithographs.

"I thought, 'Gee, I could just paint the wildlife and make a simpler statement, in a way.' It was too late to enter the federal duck stamp contest that year, so I entered the state contest in California," he said.

Actually, Steiner's first attempt at a duck stamp painting, showing a pair of pintails, had a serious error — the duck he thought was a hen was actually a male in summer eclipse plumage, when the drakes lose their bright colors for several weeks. By the time he was finished with the work he had realized his mistake, but he entered it anyway. It came in second, strengthening his resolve to do better.

The next year, 1981, Steiner won the California contest with an acrylic of two canvasbacks landing in a marsh; compared with his recent work, the painting is lackluster, although the birds are well-rendered. But the win brought acclaim and a degree of independence to Steiner.

"It was great. In 1981, there was probably more attention for winning a state that wasn't a first of state than there is now — today, the first of states have taken so many of the collectors that more people in California will probably buy the 1989 Rhode Island first of state than will buy the California stamp this year. In 1981 there were only about twenty states with stamps, so collecting them all was not impossible," Steiner said. "It was a tremendous response. At every show I went to, people would come up to get the print. It was instant celebrity. I gave up freelance magazine illustrating right away, because I never did like that very much. I gave up the teaching more slowly, and I think I gave my last class in 1986."

Fired with enthusiasm, Steiner produced a number of state and federal entries over the next two years. The results were dismal, but one experience changed his style for the better.

"In 1982 and 1983 I entered quite a few competitions, and didn't win anything. But it was in 1983 that I went to see the federal duck stamp judging in person, in Washington. I saw that almost everybody was painting on Masonite. I was painting on watercolor paper, so all my acrylics looked like watercolors — they were transparent, they didn't have the impact. So in 1984 I went to using board, and got the much crisper, harder look."

Armed with his new technique, Steiner began winning: Nevada in 1984, against a record-breaking field of 314 artists; Michigan in 1985; Florida in 1986; California in 1987; more in 1988 and 1989. Steiner attributes some of his wins not just to his method of painting sharp, detailed ducks, but to a compositional formula he developed — showing the birds in flight, with the drake in front displaying its back, and the hen to the rear, showing her underside. It is a tricky pose to render lifelike, and combined with Steiner's strong backlighting and highly realistic landscapes, it caught the judges' eye time after time.

Steiner liked the composition for a number of reasons. "I used to

A female green-winged teal preens as her mate stands watch in the 1939–40 federal design by Lynn Bogue Hunt Sr.

A solitary Canada goose on a rocky
shore dominates the 1989 Indiana
design, by Kansas artist Ann C.
Dohoney.

*"Blue" geese rise above marsh
vegetation in the 1955–56 federal
design by Stanley Stearns, done in ink
and pencil, then released as an etching
in print form. Ten each of Stearns'
three federal designs were hand-
colored by the artist, making them
exceedingly valuable on the collectors'
market.*

107

A commercial artist who turned his observations while hunting into art, Harvey Dean Sandstrom won the 1954–55 federal contest with his depiction of two ring-necked ducks.

Backlighting picks up the faint chestnut collar that gives the male ring-necked duck its name, in Paul Bridgeford's 1988 Georgia design (below). Most waterfowl hunters call this bird the "ring-bill," and certainly that field mark is more noticeable at a distance.

teach design, and the first sentence of the design textbook said 'Repetition is the basis of coherency in design.' That design has a lot of repetitious elements that create the coherency, and yet it shows off both sides of the species. The drake is the one you want to see the back of, where all the color is. It was an amazingly obvious, beautiful concept that no one had ever nailed down before."

That design is a theme through a number of Steiner's stamps, including the 1988 New Hampshire painting. But another, no less important, trademark is his use of actual locations as backgrounds for his state designs.

"Where in the federal duck stamp you probably have to have a generalized background that could be anywhere, when you're getting down to one state it's nice to have a landscape that epitomizes the waterfowl habitat in that state. People there are going to respond to that, and I enjoy painting landscapes." Steiner's Nevada 1984 — "Pintails at Stillwater" — was the first to feature such a background, actually a composite landscape ("a melange of three different photographs, but it has the look of a particular spot," the artist said).

Breakers smash on the rocks in the 1957–58 federal design by Jackson M. Abbott, showing two common eider males in flight.

The Creation of a Duck Stamp

Rhode Island's first of state in 1989 was a Steiner painting of canvasbacks at Pettaquamscutt Cove, a small estuary off Narragansett Bay. It is typical of the tightly rendered paintings that have made Steiner the winningest duck stamp artist in the country.

Steiner's first step is to roughly sketch compositional ideas. "I start with just images from my head, birds I've seen in the wild, other duck stamps, all the photographs I've seen — all that's in my head." He may do ten or more such drawings, looking for the elusive combination of pose, composition and action that may spell a winner. In Rhode Island's case, he quickly discarded a number of concepts — birds landing, birds starting to take off.

"I didn't like the composition," he said. "With a duck stamp, everything has to work together, but the first thing to me is the composition. If it's not there, why do the rest?" Steiner finally hit on one that rang true, of a pair of cans gliding in, wings back and feet dropped, a moment or two away from splash-down. "The sketch is fairly crude, and the birds are in a slightly awkward version of the position they finally got into. There's no background or anything, but I realized I had a good idea."

Referring to some of the 5,000 or more photographs he's taken, as

Hunters hide behind trees in a flooded bottomland as they decoy a small flock, in the 1986 Arkansas design "Black Swamp Mallards," by noted painter John Cowan.

well as prepared museum specimens, Steiner began refining his concept sketch. He's always careful not to rely on the stuffed birds too heavily for form and shape. "The biggest problem with taxidermy is that it's *always* wrong — it's just an approximation, and that's why you have to know the bird," he explained. Generally, Steiner only uses specimens for reference to flight details like wings or feathers, which are difficult to capture well on film.

With a carefully done pencil drawing of the birds finished, Steiner transferred the image of the canvasbacks to a Masonite panel, prepared with a ground of toned, gray gesso. "I use a toned background instead of white because acrylics are so transparent that painting on white is very difficult. But gray is very dull and deadening, so I'll mask off different areas and paint flat colors underneath as a base coat. . . . Then I'll do a fairly detailed drawing on the board in 2H pencil that will indicate all the major differences in light and dark, from one shape to another, all the turning edges. I was taught the Old Master technique of using burnt sienna for an underpainting, like Leonardo Da Vinci's 'St. Jerome with a Lion'."

Using a purplish tone of burnt sienna, Steiner does a complete

Canada geese were the subject for Minnesotan Jim Killen's 1984 Pennsylvania stamp and print. Two years later, the state switched from commissioning the stamp art to holding a contest; in 1989, it further narrowed the selection process by restricting the contest to state residents only.

111

Arkansas's print and stamp program
has been consistently successful for the
state Game and Fish Commission;
"Bois D'Arc Pintails," by Larry
Hayden, for example, brought in
nearly half a million dollars in stamp
sales and a percentage of print revenue
in 1984.

New York's designs — such as the 1988 painting of a pintail flock by Richard Plasschaert — always shows man's impact on the environment, whether in the form of a plowed field and barn, or man-made wood duck boxes.

113

value study on the board. "Acrylics are so transparent by nature that you don't have to use anything to make them a perfect glazing media. It takes a little bit more time, but the results are worth it."

Only then does Steiner begin the actual painting, laying in color glazes to build up depth and form. To do a small 6½-by-9-inch duck stamp takes about three weeks of working six hours a day, six days a week; a larger 13-by-18-inch piece takes roughly five weeks.

The Remarque Headache

Actually, the bulk of the work may still lie ahead; signing, numbering and remarquing each print. While at first blush a year like 1989, when Steiner did four state designs, might seem like a key to easy living, it means hundreds of hours working on prints. In most of the editions Steiner does, about 100 prints get a remarque — a small original pencil drawing or painting in the margin. To do 100 remarques, Steiner will create roughly ten basic designs of the species in different poses. Then, for each remarque, he changes details like back-

A banded mallard erupts from the water with another drake in the 1985 Arkansas print by Ken Carlson, whose oils are rapidly gaining him a reputation at the front of North American wildlife art.

*Spare in its execution, Walter Bohl's
1943–44 etching of a wood duck pair is
an artistic exercise in minimalism.*

grounds, so that each is a unique piece of art. Steiner has considered not doing remarques, but with a backlog of three or four years in requests for his paintings, he realizes they are often the only way the average buyer has of acquiring one of his originals.

Ron Louque, who designed the first of state stamp for Virginia in 1988, was astounded when officials from that state told him he would be doing 900 remarques — 550 in pencil and 350 in color. "This last year I haven't been doing much of anything," Louque said, "just Virginia remarques. It's really been a task, I'll tell you. A few wouldn't have been so bad, 100 or so, but this thing took up my whole time." In all, remarquing took up the better part of eight or nine months, and cut seriously into the time Louque had to paint.

Most artists remarque the way Steiner does, using a few basic designs and changing them slightly for each print. Christopher White goes to more trouble on the expensive color remarques, even though it plays hob with his schedule. "The pencils go pretty quick, but the paintings take me maybe three or four hours a piece. With color remarques, I tend to make them little scenes, as opposed to just the duck. Most of the time I'll have more than one waterfowl in it, with a full background, foliage, real detailed reflections on the water. It wreaks havoc on the galleries that are waiting for these pieces. On the other hand, once people get them I've all kinds of good response, and additional remarque orders," White said.

CHAPTER FOUR

The Business of Duck Stamps

The selection of a new federal duck stamp winner is national news, flashed across the United States by wire services. States invest hundreds of thousands of dollars promoting and advertising their programs. Limited edition prints can make small fortunes for artists and publishers.

Collectors have made duck stamps into the multi-million dollar business that they are today. The value placed on some collections is astronomical; one unique set of federal prints and stamps owned by Ducks Unlimited is said to be worth nearly a quarter of a million dollars. The 1972 Iowa print by Maynard Reece, only the second first of state in the nation (and only issued in a 500-print series) may be the most valuable of the state offerings: as much as $7,000 a print.

Clearly, duck stamps are *big* business.

Ironically, the federal government, which started the whole ball rolling in 1934, has stayed studiously out of the hype. The U.S. Fish and Wildlife Service uses the winning federal artwork to create the stamp, but almost everything else — the prints, the medallions, the spinoffs — are left to the artist. While the duck stamp office charges a royalty for products that use the image of the stamp, with its inscription, the artist

Previous page The 1988 New Hampshire stamp and print — buffleheads by Robert Steiner — was available in a wide variety of editions, including one signed by both the governor and the artist. Through such marketing strategies, states are trying to maintain or expand their sales in the face of projected declines in the print market.

Artists who designed the earlier federal stamp could expect only a modest return for their efforts. John Ruthven, who did the 1960–61 family of redheads, below, sold about 400 prints — a fraction of today's demand for a federal print.

keeps all rights to his original painting — a situation that can be a financial bonanza, especially for limited edition prints. The 1988–89 winner, Dan Smith, signed and numbered 20,000 of them, selling for as high as $1,800 for a print accompanied by a solid gold medallion. In the past decade, the federal winners have each grossed something on the order of $1 million.

Almost as much attention is given to state stamps, especially first of states — and as the number of state duck stamp programs edges toward 50, interest understandably concentrates on the dwindling inaugurals. Tiny Rhode Island, which offered its first of state in 1989, expected to make hundreds of thousands of dollars on that premier edition — a welcome chunk of cash for any wildlife department, but especially so in a state with such a small agency and budget.

To go from the idea to the first day of sale takes time and effort in any state. The proposal for a Rhode Island duck stamp had actually been advanced several years earlier, by a group of state waterfowl hunters, mostly Ducks Unlimited members.

"They met with us and developed proposed legislation for a stamp program," recalled James Chadwick, who as the deputy director of wildlife for the state spearheads the stamp program. "We could not convince the administration that we had at that time of the importance of the program, and the funding it would bring in. States go through cycles, where they don't want to put in any bills that will generate

Roland H. Clark's original version of the 1938–39 federal showed a flock of pintails, which was cropped to just two.

The 1952–53 federal design (left) focuses on a pair of harlequin ducks, and was created by John H. Dick.

"From Beyond the North Wind" was the title of Jack Murray's painting of two snow geese, done for the 1947–48 federal stamp.

121

revenue; other times, they'll go on a roll because yes, people will support them."

With state support lacking, the idea died for a time. It was resurrected in 1987 through the happy juncture of a state legislator and a college professor.

"There were changes in the state house and in the department — very positive toward land acquisition and open space protection, wetlands and so forth," Chadwick said. In the meantime, University of Rhode Island professor Chester Hickox, who was interested in this program, was teaching a class that included state Representative Christine Callahan.

"Hickox started a special project with a group of students, to investigate duck stamp programs. They got their statistics together and drafted a bill and brought it to us. We already had the OK to do something, so we took it from there," he said. With the Rhode Island Department of Fish and Wildlife working with the governor's office to ensure administration support, Callahan introduced the bill to the legislature in early 1988, where it passed.

The road was not always smooth, nor the public uniformly supportive. One small, vocal group of sportsmen, opposed to any further license increases, lobbied the state house successfully to have a provision inserted in the bill that, while making the stamp mandatory for waterfowl hunting in Rhode Island, required the state to supply the $7.50 stamp free to anyone with a valid hunting license — thus cutting the amount of money that could be raised for wetlands conservation.

With the legislation in place authorizing the program, the state convened a review committee to select the artist. Because Rhode Island's wildlife agency has such a small staff, the state opted for bid proposals rather than a contest, which is time- and labor-intensive to run. The committee decided to limit eligibility to only canvasbacks — a decision based as much on economics as esthetics, Chadwick said.

"(Canvasbacks) are a very collectible item . . . we talked to a lot of the people about what's very collectible right now, and canvasbacks are one of the species that are very, very popular. Mallards are also, but there are so many mallard prints out there, plus the mallard isn't all that popular right here, because it's becoming a nuisance duck. We thought about black ducks, because they are typical New England ducks, but they aren't as collectible. So we figured we'd kick off with a popular bird that's very pretty, very visible. It had to have a Rhode Island theme to it — a lighthouse, something people could identify with Rhode Island," Chadwick said.

Perhaps the biggest concern of the review committee was the royalty rates and marketing plans submitted by prospective publishers. The eventual winner was Steiner Prints, operated by San Francisco duck stamp artist Robert Steiner. Typical of modern duck stamp marketing strategies, his painting, "Canvasbacks at Pettaquamscutt Cove," was issued in a wide variety of editions, at a wide variety of prices. At the low end of the scale were the stamps themselves ($7.50, and the only item sold by the state itself), and regular prints with mint stamps, retailing for $142.50. For twice that price a buyer got the same print and stamp, but with a gold-plated medallion of the stamp. The executive edition, for more than $300, included a hand-colored etching; only 300 in this edition were produced.

Barrow's goldeneye, a common
western diving duck, was chosen by
the Alaska Department of Fish and
Game as the subject of its 1989 stamp.
The contest for the design attracted 61
entries from 22 states, and was won by
Michigan artist Richard Timm, who
depicted a pair in a coastal marsh.

Previous page The wake of a passing,
but hidden, goose adds tension to
Robert Bateman's 1987 painting
"Pride of Autumn," the first release of
the National Fish and Wildlife
Foundation. Created by Congress, the
foundation raises money for
conservation work. (© Robert
Bateman, courtesy Mill Pond Press)

*Mist obscures the hills in the 1987
Washington design, a highly detailed
portrait of three canvasbacks by Seattle
artist Ray Nichol.*

Framed with a mint stamp and a gold medallion, the color-remarqued 1987 governor's edition New Hampshire design set a trend now picked up by other states.

(Opposite) Increasingly, the federal duck stamps are being licensed for use on a wide variety of collectible items, including this set of gold-plated ingots produced by The Franklin Mint; each ingot bears a reproduction of one of the 55 federal stamps.

The most expensive Rhode Island offering was the governor's edition — a print signed by Steiner and Governor Edward D. DiPrete with a color remarque, mint stamp and a special governor's stamp. The idea of a governor's edition first appeared in New Hampshire in 1987 with another Steiner print. The response, Steiner said, was tremendous. "It's really caught on with the collectors." Two years later, prints from that first governor's edition were being offered for resale at almost $3,000.

Long before the prints and stamps went on sale, Steiner and the department were getting phone calls from dealers and collectors trying to lock in orders. That kind of interest means excellent sales, and Rhode Island's first of state was expected to produce between $640,000 and $1 million in royalties for the state. For Steiner, it meant plenty of work — more than 400 color and pencil remarques to execute, at a time when he had hundreds of prints from three other states to do as well. "It will take three to six months to do all those remarques, so I'll probably lose half the year to painting," Steiner said.

With wetlands conservation such a pressing concern, most states have more ways to spend duck stamp money than money itself. Rhode Island was no different. Because the entire state is considered a critical area in the North American Waterfowl Management Plan (in large part a recovery program for the declining black duck) much of the money will go toward conserving crucial black duck habitat. Pettaquamscutt Cove, the estuary featured in Steiner's painting, is one such area about to receive federal protection, while state money will be channeled to preserving salt ponds and freshwater marshes. One area, the Galilee Bird Sanctuary, is a former salt marsh that had its tidal flow cut during construction of a road in the 1950s. Now almost completely taken over by invasive phragmites reeds, which are poor wildlife habitat, the sanctuary may be converted back to salt marsh with the help of duck stamp money. In all, more than 3,000 acres statewide are being eyed for preservation or enhancement, thanks to the stamp program.

Increasingly, manufacturers have been asking to incorporate duck stamp designs in their products as a way to help sales. But Joseph Brendan Murphy, manager of the federal duck stamp licensing and marketing program, said that almost all of the companies also have a strong environmental commitment, and view the duck stamp as a way to act on that commitment. "So we are a natural for them," he said.

Even though the artist retains rights to the painting, it is up to the duck stamp office to license products that reproduce the actual stamp — the engraved design with the inscription that says "Migratory Bird Hunting and Conservation Stamp," and the price. While the duck stamp office is obviously wary of any licensing arrangement that would place the stamp in an unfavorable light, or be a party to bad taste, Murphy said situations of that sort simply haven't arisen so far.

"I've seen a real sensitivity to taste," he said. "This is their government, their Fish and Wildlife Service, and their product. It reflects on them."

The variety of products that have featured the federal duck stamp covers a wide range, Murphy said: T-shirts, collector's knives, belt buckles, gold ingot sets, $10,000 shotguns, decorative decoys with the stamp inscribed on the base, "wall plaques of all varieties," desk boxes and lapel pins. Beam distillers produced a series of ceramic bourbon decanters modeled after the winning images, and the National Fish and Wildlife Foundation — itself a federally created group that produces its own stamp — markets a collector card series of the federal design, with a mint stamp affixed to it.

Not every joint effort between the duck stamp office and private industry results in a product. In 1989, the U.S. Fish and Wildlife Service announced that, for the first time, federal duck stamps would be available at no additional cost through dealers affiliated with the Remington Arms Co., a manufacturer of hunting guns and equipment. Previously, the stamps were available over the counter only through post offices.

The 1989 Arizona stamp, showing a pair of cinnamon teal, displays artist Robert Steiner's highly successful compositional formula — both birds in flight, with the male's back and female's underside toward the viewer. That way, Steiner is able to show the most colorful parts of the bird while infusing the painting with movement.

The tide of licensing requests keeps growing; in a month-long period in early 1989, Murphy fielded 60 different ideas. "The limitation is clearly the creative imagination of the product manufacturer," he said. One company is trying — thus far unsuccessfully — to figure out a way to imprint the duck stamp design on telescopic gun sights. Others face a different problem, because the stamp carries both a price and an expiration date, both of which must be faithfully reproduced on any licensed product. If the product has a different selling price, as it usually does, it can cause confusion. "We have shelf-dated the item with the expiration date, and it has the price $12.50 on it — but the shirt is $29, or whatever," Murphy said.

Because the duck stamp office collects a royalty on product sales, usually ten percent, licensing means additional money for waterfowl conservation. Murphy estimated that the royalties amounted to between $50,000 and $75,000 each year since 1984, but until recently the duck stamp office was content to simply accept or reject marketing ideas that came in from manufacturers. Now, the office is actively soliciting new licensing ideas and working closely with the producers, so that total should rise in the years ahead.

Sometimes, mistakes aren't noticed until it's too late. It was only after judges had selected Robert Knutson's painting of blue-winged teal to be the 1986 Pennsylvania stamp that officials noticed that the artist had neglected to give the drake primary wing feathers, which would ordinarily extend out over the tail.

Not everyone is in favor of licensed products. Carl Graybill, the Pennsylvania stamp coordinator, worries that mass reproduction of the design cheapens its value as art, and he has turned down requests for use of the state's stamps. One recently was from a reputable conservation group that wanted to sell lapel pins enameled with the winning design.

"I gave it quite a bit of thought, but my personal feeling is that I don't like to see a piece of quality wildlife art that's intended for a fine art print and collectible stamp to appear on all kinds of trinkets and gadgets," he said. "I don't think it's worth what you're going to do to downgrade the program for $5,000 or $10,000 in additional revenues. We have all the reproduction rights to those paintings, and we could do with them what we want, but I have a problem from the standpoint of degrading the work of an artist."

(Opposite) Ron Ferkol led a field of 50 entries to win the 1987 Missouri contest with his painting of a pair of pintails. (Bottom) A selection of Wisconsin's long-running stamp series.

Despite its wide range and handsome appearance, the ring-necked duck has only been featured on duck stamps a handful of times. One of them is this, the 1985 Michigan design by Robert Steiner.

131

*A pair of mallards, painted by David
Chapple, grace the 1988 Utah stamp
and print.*

*Wood ducks, one of the most popular
species of waterfowl, dominate "The
Suitors," the 1989 U.S. National Fish
and Wildlife Foundation's design.
Painted by British native John Seerey-
Lester, the print came in three editions
— regular, medallion and executive,
the last of which carried a mint stamp,
a signed stamp and an original
etching.*

The Duck Stamp Legacy

Just as the success of the federal duck stamp gave rise to the state programs, so too has the continuing popularity of waterfowl stamps in general brought about the introduction of stamps for almost every conservation purpose imaginable.

Many states now sell stamps to raise money for nongame wildlife, for trout and salmon, for upland game or habitat in general. Often, such state-sponsored stamps are, like most duck stamps, a type of hunting license. Not so with stamps put out by conservation groups like the International Quail Foundation, the Smallmouth Bass Foundation, the Ruffed Grouse Society, the Waterfowl Habitat Alliance of Texas or the Pennsylvania Federation of Sportsmen's Clubs, which are designed simply to raise money. Next to the federal duck stamp, the oldest fund-raising stamp series is that issued each year by the National Wildlife Federation. The first set, issued in 1938, was painted by Federation founder "Ding" Darling — the man who also painted the first federal duck stamp.

The National Fish and Wildlife Foundation, created in 1984 by Congress as a public-private partnership to raise funds for conserva-

Mist-clouded hills and a fallen birch tree frame a pintail pair in Robert Leslie's 1987 Pennsylvania design.

tion, also issues stamps and prints each year. The first, in 1987, was a
Canada goose by Robert Bateman, followed the next year by mallards
painted by Maynard Reece — proof that, even when an edition is not
strictly a "duck stamp" (the NFWF's work benefits all wildlife),
waterfowl are still the safest way to reach a large market.

Canada has come late to the conservation stamp arena. Its first
nationwide habitat stamp was released in 1985, and while it, like the
NFWF series, is not strictly a duck stamp, it has featured two
waterfowl paintings by Bateman and one by J. Fenwick Lansdowne.
In 1988 Quebec issued a first of province habitat stamp, a luminous
ruffed grouse by Jean-Luc Grondin.

*Backed by a heavy advertising
campaign and tremendous interest
among first of the state collectors,
Virginia's 1988 inaugural design by
Ron Louque was a rapid sell-out.
Many states experience high sales for
their first stamp, then see a sag as
collector interest turns elsewhere, to
another first of state.*

The Future of Duck Stamps

Since the mid–1970s, and especially through the 1980s, the duck
stamp market has been in a state of almost constant, rapid growth.
But even as waterfowl stamps and prints reach new heights of
popularity, those most closely associated with the art form wonder
what the future will hold.

135

Edward Morris won the 1962–63 federal competition with a black-and-white wash painting of pintails, then created a drypoint etching of the image from which the print was made. It was Morris' second federal win in a row — the only time an artist has won the prestigious contest in back-to-back years.

"I think the market's becoming pretty gluttonized," said Nancy Schneider, the marketing specialist in charge of New York's stamp program. "We want people to go beyond just collecting the 'first of states'." New York has tried to set itself apart from the crowd by commissioning top-name artists like Robert Bateman, and pushing the conservation message — something that frequently gets lost in the shuffle in many states.

"From an artistic perspective, the programs that will do better are the ones that aren't living by the rules, so to speak, that were established long ago — in other words, two ducks squatting on a pond, or something along those lines," Schneider said. "We have to branch out to appeal to a broader audience than perhaps we've been appealing to before, getting other people caught up in the significance of the artwork and what it means to conservation, as opposed to just liking a certain species, or wanting a particular picture on the wall.

"From an individual state perspective, people are going to have to get wiser about trying to market and promote, and really establish a mind-set about their particular series of prints, associate it with a concept of what the state is trying to do for conservation. . . . New

York's been trying to get people involved in the broad-based perspective of what a print purchase means, in terms of the habitat work we're doing in New York and up in Canada."

Schneider also foresees a serious drop in print sales.

"Yes, I think there probably will come a time when we will have exhausted ways of getting new blood into the program. It's not as easy as it was in the beginning, when it was a novel idea. That's why people have to be concerned, not about selling a great big first of state edition, but about how things level off after the fact. New York was very much part of that big dip.... The competition is going to make people try to do something different, or position the product in a way that will attract a different group of people that haven't been saturated before."

Pennsylvania is taking a different tack toward preserving its print sales: the native son approach. Beginning with the 1989 contest, that state closed the competition to all but Pennsylvania artists.

"The main reason we decided to go that route was to raise additional revenues for the program," said Graybill, the waterfowl stamp coordinator. "We'll be able to promote the program at a higher level — be able to have the artist on hand at art shows or wherever it would be appropriate, have him meet the public and sign stamps and promote the program." Since the state began open competition in 1986, Pennsylvania artists have always been finalists, but have never won the contest — a fact that Graybill believes cuts into print sales within the state.

"We're going to lose whatever print sales occur within the out-of-state winner's home region, but I think it's going to offset by increased sales here by having a Pennsylvania artist do it," he said.

Graybill predicts many states will be taking similar approaches, making their marketing program more insular, targeting residents of their own states rather than relying on nationwide sales. "You're going to have states get involved in a maintenance program, whereby they're selling prints to people within their states, with minimal participation out of that state. That's what's going to carry the program. We've seen that in Pennsylvania: we sold 8,000 prints the first year, and since then it's been anywhere from 2,200 to 3,000. We're pretty satisfied with that."

Charles Heartwell III, the coordinator of West Virginia's duck stamp program, is less sanguine. "The bonanza is about to dry up, and the people in the duck stamp business, like the print publishers, see it coming. What we're seeing with the continuing programs, with rare exceptions, is that they gradually dwindle over time, with the prints finally stabilizing at some low sales figure. We've tried to reverse that (trend) by being unique and innovative, cutting some special cooperative sales contracts, that I don't know if we'll be successful in the long haul."

Regardless of what happens to the print market, it is clear that duck stamps themselves will remain. In many states print sales are handled strictly by the winning artists, while the states, which sponsor the programs, reap most of their money from sales of stamps. As added insurance, many states require that waterfowl hunters buy the stamps as a form of licensing, thus guaranteeing a continuing market. Only a few states, like Pennsylvania, New York

Regional specialties are stamp favorites. In Vermont (top and middle), wood ducks and black ducks are common migrants, while in the Central Flyway, white-fronted geese are more typical. Jim Killen painted both Vermont stamps, while Marion Tiollion painted the South Dakota image. (Vermont stamps © State of Vermont)

and Georgia, have voluntary stamps, and even some of those are being reconsidered. The Georgia Legislature was to consider making its stamp mandatory starting in 1989, while North Carolina, which had a voluntary stamp for several years, made it a requirement for hunting beginning in 1988.

Pennsylvania usually sells less than 15,000 stamps each year, in a state that has three times that many waterfowl hunters — a significant revenue loss. The stamp was made voluntary, Graybill said, because making it mandatory would have required legislative approval — a time-consuming process, and one that would have faced an uncertain future. "At the time there would have been some reluctance, I'm sure, to creating a mandatory duck stamp, but I kind of wish now we had gone that route," Graybill said. Selling 50,000 stamps a year — a reasonable expectation if they were required — would mean "a quarter of a million dollars a year that we could have in addition to print sales of $125,000. We could do a lot with that money," he said. However, consideration of a mandatory stamp will probably have to wait for the next general license increase, sometime in the next three years.

Heartwell sees a strength in the stamp market as well, although for a different reason. "Stamp revenues are going to hold up pretty well.

Intense blue contrasts with the green head of the drake goldeneye in Cynthie Fisher's 1988 Ohio stamp and print.

© Cynthie Fisher

The philatelics people follow stamps closely, and if you have a reputable program with a piece of reasonable quality art each year, they get locked into buying your stamp — and that's a far easier market to get into than the print market."

Along with dramatic changes in marketing and promotion, duck stamp art itself is sure to continue to evolve, as it has since the early days of black-and-white etchings. Robert Steiner, one of the most successful duck stamp artists in the country, sees the growing reliance on a photographic look as sure bet for the future.

"Artistically, I think more people will strive for a greater degree of realism, making it more like a painting and a little less like a design. People will have to try new things. It's funny — everyone knows what a duck stamp is, but no one's ever written down a description of what makes one thing look like a duck stamp and other things not. But the judges will always say, 'Well, this one looks like a duck stamp, but this one looks like an exhibition piece.' Possibly the look of the exhibition piece, as it were, will enter into it in the future," Steiner said.

Five-time federal winner Maynard Reece, who has seen the duck stamp market explode since he first won the contest, refuses to speculate on what the future holds.

Wood ducks fly past nest boxes, protected with sheet-metal predator guards, in the 1986 Maine design by David Maass. Maass, one of the most popular waterfowl artists in the country, was contracted by the state to create its initial three stamps, beginning with the 1984 first of state.

Only eight or nine artists submitted designs for the then little-known federal contest in 1948. Roger Preuss won with his wash of goldeneyes in flight, which appeared on the 1949–50 stamp.

Shovelers, teal relatives with outsized beaks, have only appeared twice on duck stamps — in this 1945–46 federal design by Owen J. Gromme, and on the 1982 Nevada stamp by Richard Timm.

Many authorities credit Joseph Knap, who painted a watercolor of greater scaup for the 1937–38 federal stamp, with issuing the first print of the stamp image. Others point to Richard Bishop, who created the previous year's stamp, with starting the print series.

Using watercolor and gouache, James Partee Jr. painted a pair of Canada geese in a lily-bedecked pond to win the 1987 Georgia contest.

"I would be the last person to want to project any idea of what the future will be. It's been such a wild market. I had misgivings twenty or thirty years ago that it was practically done, and it's mushroomed ever since," he said, laughing. "So I just have no idea of what's going to happen to it."

Wood ducks fly through a birch forest in the 1988 Pennsylvania print and stamp, painted by Iowa artist John Heidersbach.

Acknowledgments

It is with sincere gratitude that I thank the many people who assisted in assembling the illustrations and information in this book. In particular, I wish to acknowledge the help of the following people: Byron G. Webster of the American Museum of Wildlife Art, Frontenac, Minnesota, who graciously allowed the Museum's collection of federal prints to be photographed; Norma Opgrand and Joseph Brendan Murphy at the federal duck stamp office; artists Robert Steiner, Maynard Reece, Christopher White, Arthur Eakin and Ron Louque, for their enthusiasm and cooperation; Dave Dick at the California Department of Fish and Game; Tom Keefe of the Minnesota Department of Natural Resources; Nancy Schneider of the New York Department of Environmental Conservation; Carl Graybill of the Pennsylvania Game Commission; James Chadwick of the Rhode Island Department of Fish and Wildlife; Charles M. Heartwell III of the West Virginia Department of Natural Resources; Mill Pond Press, Voyageur Art, Petersen Prints and Larry Grisham, all of whom supplied transparencies for this book. Thanks also to the many state duck stamp coordinators and Ducks Unlimited chapter directors who set aside their busy schedules to answer questions and locate transparencies.

PHOTO CREDITS: © Joe McDonald pages 11, 12, 29; © Scott Weidensaul pages 22, 38, 39.

Appendix to Federal Duck Stamps

The federal duck stamp is still the standard against which all others are measured – the longest-running and most prestigious issue of its kind. Here, in synopsis form, is a rundown of all 55 federal designs.

1934–35

Title and medium: "Mallards Dropping In"; ink.
Species and setting: Mallard pair landing in marsh.
Artist: J.N. "Ding" Darling, then the head of the U.S. Biological Survey, which administered the duck stamp program. Darling's ink drawing (one of three preliminary designs he submitted for consideration) is done in the same cartooning style that had made him a nationally recognized artist.
Print: At least one edition of roughly 300 etchings was produced.
Stamp: Face value, $1. Number printed, 5,029,600; number sold, 635,001, raising $635,001.
Notes: Darling was allowed to purchase the first stamp. The print was not issued until several years after the stamp release.

1935–36

Title and medium: None; black and white wash.
Species and setting: Three canvasbacks in flight over marsh.
Artist: Frank W. Benson, famous for his etchings, especially of waterfowl subjects.
Print: A first (and probably only) edition of about 100 unnumbered prints was made from an etched plate.
Stamp: Face value, $1. Number printed, 2,089,920; number sold, 448,204. Money raised, $448,204.
Notes: The stamp, printed in beautiful rose lake ink, and the print are the rarest in the long federal series.

1936–37

Title and medium: "Coming In"; etching.
Species and setting: Three Canada geese in flight, shown against a cloudy backdrop.
Artist: Richard E. Bishop, who, like Benson, was a noted etcher.
Print: The edition was not numbered, and it is unknown how many prints it contained.
Stamp: Face value, $1. Number printed, 1,451,968; number sold, 603,623. Money raised, $603,623.
Notes: Like Benson the year before, Bishop designed the art at the invitation of J.N. Darling.

1937–38

Title and medium: None; monochromatic watercolor wash.
Species and setting: Greater scaup flying over Great South Bay, Long Island.
Artist: Joseph D. Knap of New York City.
Print: 260 unnumbered prints.
Stamp: Face value, $1. Number printed, 2,289,504; number sold 783,039. Money raised, $783,039.
Notes: Although there is disagreement on the point, it is generally believed that Knap was the first duck stamp artist to issue a print of his design; Darling, Benson and Bishop then followed suit.

1938–39

Title and medium: Unknown; etching.
Species and setting: Pintail pair landing in wetlands.
Artist: Roland H. Clark.
Print: A single edition of roughly 300 etchings.
Stamp: Face value, $1. Number printed, 2,172,576; number sold, 1,002,715. Money raised, $1,002,715.
Notes: The artist's original design was an etching that showed five birds, but the plate was cropped before the stamp was made, reducing the number of birds to just two.

1939–40

Title and medium: Unknown; graphite pencil.
Species and setting: Green-winged teal pair at rest.
Artist: Lynn Bogue Hunt, a nationally known wildlife illustrator.
Print: Two editions of unknown size, done in stone lithography.
Stamp: Face value, $1. Number printed, 2,240,000; number sold, 1,111,561. Money raised, $1,111,561.

1940–41

Title and medium: None; black and white wash.
Species and setting: Two black ducks flying over windswept wild rice.
Artist: Francis Lee Jaques.

Print: Three editions of approximately 260 stone lithographs.
Stamp: Face value, $1. Number printed, 2,800,784; number sold, 1,260,810. Money raised, $1,260,80.

1941–42

Title and medium: "Ruddy Ducks"; tempera/wash painting.
Species and setting: Pair of ruddy ducks with young.
Artist: Edwin R. Kalmbach, Colorado.
Print: Two editions of unknown size; the first edition had a reversed image.
Stamp: Face value, $1. Number printed, 1,954,960; number sold 1,439,967. Money raised, $1,439,967.
Notes: Kalmbach was a U.S. Fish and Wildlife Service biologist. By showing a pair of adult ducks with young, the painting leaves the impression that male ruddy ducks help care for the chicks. They do not, but males will often associate with females throughout the breeding season, trying to mate with them.

1942–43

Title and medium: "American Widgeon"; drypoint etching.
Species and setting: A flock of American wigeon (note that the spelling of the bird's name has changed since the stamp was issued) in a marsh.
Artist: Alden L. Ripley.
Print: A single edition of unknown size.
Stamp: Face value, $1. Number printed, 3,106,992: number sold, 1,383,629. Money raised, $1,383,629.

1943–44

Title and medium: "Federal Duck Stamp Design – 1943"; drypoint etching.
Species and setting: A male and female wood duck in flight against clouds.
Artist: Walter E. Bohl.
Print: Two editions; the first edition consisted of 290 prints, with an unknown number in the second edition.
Stamp: Face value, $1. Number printed, 3,022,320; number sold, 1,169,352. Money raised, $1,169,352.

1944–45

Title and medium: "White-fronted Geese"; black and white wash.
Species and setting: Three white-fronted geese, shown closely cropped as they are landing.
Artist: Walter A. Weber, well-known illustrator and ornithologist.
Print: Like Kalmbach's ruddy ducks in 1941–42, the first edition of Weber's signed, unnumbered print was flopped, while the two subsequent editions were not.
Stamp: Face value, $1. Number printed, 3,033,632; number sold, 1,487,029. Money raised, $1,487,029.

1945–46

Title and medium: "Spoonbills"; black and white wash.
Species and setting: Three shovelers (known as "spoonbills") in flight.
Artist: Owen J. Gromme, later to become one of the deans of American wildlife art.
Print: A single edition of 250 signed prints.
Stamp: Face value, $1. Number printed, 1,948,688; number sold 1,725,505. Money raised, $1,725,505.

1946–47

Title and medium: "Redheads"; ink drawing with wash.
Species and setting: A male redhead landing to join a small swimming flock.
Artist: Robert W. Hines, who the next year was hired to administer the duck stamp program.
Print: Two editions – a first edition of roughly 300, and a second edition of 385.
Stamp: Face value, $1. Number printed, 3,334,240; number sold, 2,016,841. Money raised, $2,016,841.
Notes: Hines originally drew his design with a second flock of swimming ducks, which Fish and Wildlife officials asked him to remove. This was the first stamp to sell more than 2 million.

1947–48

Title and medium: "From Beyond the North Wind"; tempera/wash painting.
Species and setting: Two flying snow geese.
Artist: Jack Murray, Boston.
Print: A single edition of 300 unsigned prints.
Stamp: Face value, $1. Number printed, 4,419,080; number sold, 1,772,677. Money raised, $1,772,677.

1948–49

Title and medium: "Buffleheads Aloft"; wash/tempera painting.
Species and setting: Three buffleheads in flight over a choppy lake.
Artist: Maynard Reece.
Print: Four editions: A first edition of 200, a second edition of 150, a third edition of 400, and a fourth edition of 350; 25 artist's proofs were also made.
Stamp: Face value, $1. Number printed, 4,419,080; number sold, 2,127,603. Money raised, $2,127,603.

1949–50

Title and medium: "American Goldeneyes"; black and white wash.
Species and setting: A pair of goldeneye descend to quiet cove at Leech Lake, Minnesota.
Artist: Roger E. Preuss, Minnesota.

Print: A single edition of 250 unnumbered signed prints, several of them remarqued in pencil.
Stamp: Face value, $2. Number printed, 4,880,624; number sold, 1,954,734. Money raised, $3,909,468.
Notes: This was the first issue to generate more than $3 million for wetlands conservation.

1950–51

Title and medium: "Trumpeter Swans"; black and white wash.
Species and setting: Two trumpeter swans flying over a stark background of Red Rock Lakes National Wildlife Refuge in Montana, where this bird was saved from extinction.
Artist: Walter A. Weber.
Print: A first edition of 500 and a second edition 300; roughly half of the first edition were lost.
Stamp: Face value, $2. Number printed, 4,777,024; number sold, 1,903,644. Money raised, $3,807,288.
Notes: This is officially regarded as the first year for full, public competition, with 88 designs by 66 artists being submitted. It was Weber's second design in five years.

1951–52

Title and medium: "Gadwalls"; tempera.
Species and setting: Two gadwall leaping into flight.
Artist: Maynard Reece.
Print: Two editions – 250 unnumbered prints in the first, 400 in the second.
Stamp: Face value, $2. Number printed, 5,156,704; number sold 2,167,767. Money raised, $4,335,534.
Notes: This is the only federal stamp to have featured gadwall, a rather plain puddle duck. It was Reece's second win.

1952–53

Title and medium: "Harlequin Ducks"; black and white wash.
Species and setting: A pair of harlequin ducks in flight above a stormy winter coast.
Artist: John H. Dick, South Carolina.
Print: Two editions – a first edition of unknown size, and a second of 300 prints.
Stamp: Face value, $2. Number printed, 5,176,192; number sold, 2,296,628. Money raised, $4,593,256.
Notes: This is the only federal stamp to have featured the harlequin duck, an uncommon species of the West and far North.

1953–54

Title and medium: "Early Express – Blue-winged Teal"; ink wash.
Species and setting: A flock of blue-winged teal turning sharply over wind-blown reeds.

Artist: Clayton B. Seager, New York.
Print: Two editions – a first of about 250, and a second of 1,500.
Stamp: Face value, $2. Number printed, 5,577,824; number sold, 2,268,446. Money raised, $4,536,892.

1954–55

Title and medium: "Ring-necked Duck"; monochromatic watercolor.
Species and setting: Two ring-necked ducks coming in for a landing.
Artist: Harvey D. Sandstrom, Minnesota.
Print: Two editions – 250 signed, unnumbered prints in the first, 400 in the second.
Stamp: Face value, $2. Number printed, 5,239,360; number sold, 2,184,550. Money raised, $4,369,100.

1955–56

Title and medium: "Blue Geese"; ink and pencil on scratchboard.
Species and setting: Three "blue" phase snow geese climbing into the air over a marsh.
Artist: Stanley Stearns.
Print: 250 signed, unnumbered prints, in two batches – one printed in black ink, one in brown.
Stamp: Face value, $2. Number printed, 5,656,336: number sold, 2,369,940. Money raised, 4,739,880.

1956–57

Title and medium: "American Mergansers"; monochromatic watercolor.
Species and setting: Two American (now common) mergansers in flight along a river.
Artist: Edward J. Bierly.
Print: 450 signed prints in the first edition.
Stamp: Face value, $2. Number printed, unknown; number sold, 2,332,014. Money raised, $4,664,028.
Notes: This was the first year in which the government presented the winner with a special album containing a pane of mint stamps.

1957–58

Title and medium: "American Eider"; gouache.
Species and setting: Two drake eiders flying above breaking surf.
Artist: Jackson Miles Abbott.
Print: Three editions 250 prints, 500 and 1,500,
Stamp: Face value, $2. Number printed, unknown; number sold, 2,355,353. Money raised, $4,710,706.
Notes: Abbott also placed in this year's contest with a painting of a brant.

1958–59

Title and medium: "Canada Geese"; black and white wash.
Species and setting: Three Canada Geese in a cornfield watch a group of five more descending.
Artist: Leslie C. Kouba, Minnesota
Print: Two editions of unknown size.
Stamp: Face value, $2. Number printed, unknown; number sold, 2,176, 425. Money raised, $4,331,124.
Notes: This was the first year the depiction of a species was repeated. Canada Geese had appeared in 1936–37.

1959–60

Title and medium: "King Buck"; wash and watercolor.
Species and setting: A Labrador retriever (national champion King Buck of Nilo Farms), shown holding a dead mallard in his mouth against a backdrop of marsh grass and flying ducks.
Artist: Maynard Reece.
Print: Three editions – 400, 300 and 400.
Stamp: Face value, $3. Number printed, 6,108,120; number sold, 1,628,365. Money raised, $4,885,095.
Notes: The selection of a stamp showing a retriever was part of an agency-wide campaign at Fish and Wildlife to encourage the use of dogs to retrieve cripples.

1960–61

Title and medium: "Redhead Ducks"; black and white wash.
Species and setting: A male and female redhead with four newly hatched chicks.
Artist: John A. Ruthven, Ohio.
Print: 400 signed, unnumbered prints.
Stamp: Face value, $3. Number printed, 5,997,840: number sold, 1,727,534. Money raised, 5,182,602.
Notes: Despite the setting that Ruthven showed, male redheads take no part in the incubation of eggs or the care of the young, nor do males spend any appreciable amount of time with females and their young. The competing artists were instructed to illustrate the theme "Wildlife Needs Water – Preserve Wetlands."

1961–62

Title and medium: "Nine Mallards"; black and white wash.
Species and setting: A hen mallard with her eight chicks among cattails.
Artist: Edward A. Morris, Minnesota.
Print: A single edition of 250 signed prints.
Stamp: Face value, $3. Number printed, 5,987,040; number sold, 1,346,003. Money raised, $4,038,009.
Notes: The theme for the 1961–62 contest was "Habitat Produces Ducks."

1962–63

Title and medium: "Pintails"; black and white wash.
Species and setting: Two pintail drakes landing on a marsh with several diving ducks.
Artist: Edward A. Morris, Minnesota.
Print: A single edition of 250 signed prints.
Stamp: Face value, $3. Number printed, 6,634,800; number sold, 1,147,553. Money raised, $3,442,659.
Notes: Morris is the only artist to have won the federal contest two years in a row. His design is also the only federal stamp to show more than one species of waterfowl, although the divers are a minor part of the image.

1963–64

Title and medium: "American Brant"; black and white wash.
Species and setting: Two brant descend on coastal waters with a lighthouse in the background.
Artist: Edward J. Bierly, Virginia.
Print: 675 signed, unnumbered prints.
Stamp: Face value, $3. Number printed, 7,495,080; number sold, 1,455,486. Money raised, $4,366,458.
Notes: "Ducks for Recreation" was the theme for this year's contest.

1964–65

Title and medium: "Nene High Among the Lava Flows"; black and white wash and gouache.
Species and setting: Two nene (Hawaiian geese) grazing on grass growing between black lava flows.
Artist: Stanley Stearns.
Print: Two editions: 665 in the first and 100 in the second, including 10 hand-colored prints.
Stamp: Face value, $3. Number printed, 5,298,000; number sold, 1,573,155. Money raised, $4,697,580.
Notes: Like the trumper swans on the 1950–51 stamp, the nene is a protected species that cannot be hunted.

1965–66

Title and medium: "Canvasbacks"; black and white wash.
Species and setting: Three drake canvasbacks skimming rough water.
Artist: Ron Jenkins, Pennsylvania.
Print: 700 signed, unnumbered prints, including 10 hand-colored by Jenkins.
Stamp: Face value, $3. Number printed, 5,067,840; number sold, 1,558,755. Money raised, $4,676,265.

1966–67

Title and medium: "Whistling Swans"; black and white wash.
Species and setting: Two tundra (formerly whistling) swans flying against a conifer-lined shore.
Artist: Stanley Stearns.
Print: Two editions of 300 prints each.
Stamp: Face value, $3. Number printed, 3,668,520; number sold, 1,805,341. Money raised, $5,414,349.
Notes: This was Stearns' third win, a record matched only by Edward J. Bierly (three) and Maynard Reece (five).

1967–68

Title and medium: "Old Squaw – Tree River N.W.T."; black and white wash.
Species and setting: A pair of oldsquaw (formerly old squaw) sitting on an ice floe in Canada's Northwest Territories.
Artist: Leslie C. Kouba, Minnesota.
Print: Two versions of a single, 250-print edition.
Stamp: Face value, $3. Number printed, 4,321,200; number sold, 1,934,697. Money raised, $5,804,091.

1968–69

Title and medium: "Poised"; black and white wash.
Species and setting: A pair of hooded mergansers sitting on a fallen log just above the water.
Artist: Claremont Gale Pritchard, Nebraska.
Print: 750 numbered prints.
Stamp: Face value, $3. Number printed, 3,653,520; number sold, 1,837,139. Money raised, $5,435,262.

1969–70

Title and medium: "White-winged Scoters"; black and white wash.
Species and setting: A pair of white-winged scoters running along the water's surface, trying to get airborne.
Artist: Maynard Reece.
Print: 750 numbered prints.
Stamp: Face value, $3. Number printed, 3,717,840; number sold, 2,087,115. Money raised, $6,261,345.
Notes: This stamp set two records – the first to generate more than $6 million in sales, and the first time the same artist won the contest four times.

1970–71

Title and medium: "Ross' Geese"; watercolor.
Species and setting: Two Ross' geese, one preening, against a colorful water background.
Artist: Edward J. Bierly, Virginia.

Print: Two editions – 1,000 and 2,150. The initial 300 of the first edition were remarqued by the artist, the first time federal prints were remarqued on such a scale.

Stamp: Face value, $3. Number printed, 5,983,560; number sold, 2,420,244. Money raised, $6,960,732.

Notes: This was the first year in which artists were allowed to submit colored designs, and the first in which color stamps and prints were released. It also marked Bierly's third win.

1971–72

Title and medium: "Cinnamon Teal"; color wash.

Species and setting: Three cinnamon teal dropping in for a landing.

Artist: Maynard Reece.

Print: 950 prints, each hand-colored by a member of the Reece family.

Stamp: Face value, $3. Number printed, 6,467,520; number sold, 2,428,647. Money raised, $7,278,174.

Notes: This marked Reece's fifth and final win, to date. It was also the last print to be produced with the stone lithography technique, rather than modern photolithography.

1972–73

Title and medium: "Emperor Geese"; watercolor.

Species and setting: Two adult emperor geese landing on a pond in Alaska.

Artist: Arthur M. Cook, Minnesota.

Print: Two editions – 950 (200 remarqued) in the first, and 900 (400 remarqued) in the second.

Stamp: Face value, $5. Number printed, 8,197,320; number sold, 2,183,981. Money raised, $10,898,140.

Notes: Because of the price increase to $5, this was the first stamp to generate more than $10 million.

1973–74

Title and medium: "Stellar's Eider"; opaque watercolor.

Species and setting: A pair of Stellar's eiders, a rare arctic species, standing along a rocky shore.

Artist: Lee LeBlanc.

Print: Two editions; 1,000 numbered prints, and 600 signed, numbered prints, 300 of them remarqued.

Stamp: Face value, $5. Number printed, 6,454,080; number sold, 2,113,594. Money raised, $10,567,970.

1974–75

Title and medium: "Wood Ducks"; oil.

Species and setting: Two wood ducks rising in front of a dead tree.

Artist: David Maass.

Print: An unnumbered, unlimited single edition.

Stamp: Face value, $5. Number printed, 6,168,480; number sold, 2,190,268. Money raised, $10,951,340.

1975–76

Title and medium: "Canvasback"; watercolor.
Species and setting: A weathered canvasback decoy, with three live cans flying in the background.
Artist: James P. Fisher.
Print: 3,150 numbered prints.
Stamp: Face value, $5. Number printed, 6,258,480; number sold, 2,218,589. Money raised, $11,092,945.
Notes: With Maynard Reece's 1959–60 design of a Labrador retriever, this stands as the most unusual federal stamp, and the only time a decoy has appeared as a subject in this series. The selection caused a great deal of controversy, including unproven charges that the contest was rigged. Following Fisher's win, the contest rules were changed to require that the winning design must feature as its main subject living, native waterfowl.

1976–77

Title and medium: "Canada Geese"; ink on scratchboard.
Species and setting: A pair of Canada geese guard their four goslings.
Artist: Alderson Magee, Connecticut.
Print: 4,600 signed, numbered prints.
Stamp: Face value, $5. Number printed, 6,875,460; number sold, 2,170,194. Money raised, $10,850,970.
Notes: Magee's win is remarkable because his original art was in black and white, rather than color, which had been the standard for a number of years. The artist only started the work three days before it was due, and sent it off just 20 minutes before the midnight deadline.

1977–78

Title and medium: "Ross' Geese"; acrylic.
Species and setting: Two Ross' geese in flight just above a snowy bank.
Artist: Martin R. Murk, Wisconsin.
Print: 5,800 numbered prints.
Stamp: Face value, $5. Number printed, 13,056,960; number sold, 2,180,625. Money raised, $10,903,125.
Notes: This year, the name of the stamp was officially changed to "United States Migratory Bird Hunting *and Conservation* Stamp," to emphasize the importance that duck stamp funds play in wetlands preservation, and to encourage birders and other non-hunters to buy them.

1978–79

Title and medium: "Hooded Merganser"; opaque watercolor.
Species and setting: A drake hooded merganser, crest raised, gliding across calm blue water.
Artist: Albert Earl Gilbert, Connecticut.
Print: 7,150 prints, 1,350 of them with watercolor remarques.
Stamp: Face value, $5. Number printed, unknown; number sold,

2,196,758. Money raised, $10,983,790.
Notes: The image of a single bird was borne for the first time.

1979–80

Title and medium: "Green-winged Teal"; gouache.
Species and setting: A pair of green-winged teal shown close-up on the water.
Artist: Ken Michaelson, California.
Print: 8,500 prints. Instead of remarques, Michaelson executed a small etching that was mounted below the print with the stamp.
Stamp: Face value, $7.50. Number printed, 7,493,160; number sold, 2,209,572. Money raised, $16,571,790.
Notes: Michaelson was the winner of the 1978 California state contest the previous year, using a similar compositional formula with hooded mergansers.

1980–81

Title and medium: "Mallards"; acrylic.
Species and setting: A pair of mallards flying over a cattail marsh.
Artist: Richard W. Plasschaert, Minnesota.
Print: 12,950 numbered prints.
Stamp: Face value, $7.50. Number printed, not available; number sold, 2,103,021. Money raised, $15,772,657.
Notes: Due to increased publicity, the number of entries in this year's contest increased by nearly 1,000 over the previous year's, to 1,329.

1981–82

Title and medium: "Ruddy Ducks"; gouache.
Species and setting: A pair of ruddy ducks sitting on quiet water.
Artist: John S. Wilson, South Dakota.
Print: A single edition of 16,000 numbered prints.
Stamp: Face value, $7.50. Number printed, 7,359,000; number sold, 1,940,578. Money raised, $14,554,335.

1982–83

Title and medium: "Canvasbacks"; oil.
Species and setting: Three canvasbacks landing on a windy lake beneath a stormy sky.
Artist: David Maass, Minnesota.
Print: 22,250 prints, plus 800 signed and numbered "conservation" prints.
Stamp: Face value, $7.50. Number printed, 8,831,760; number sold, 1,926,253. Money raised, $14,446,897.

1983–84

Title and medium: "Pintails"; acrylic.
Species and setting: A pair of pintails in golden light.
Artist: Phil V. Scholer, Minnesota.
Print: 17,400 standard prints, plus a medallion edition of 6,700.
Stamp: Face value, $7.50. Number printed, unavailable; number sold, 1,867,998. Money raised, $14,009,985.
Notes: This issue marked the 50th anniversary of the federal program, an event commemorated by the special medallion edition print and a traveling duck stamp exhibit.

1984–85

Title and medium: "Wigeon"; acrylic.
Species and setting: A pair of American wigeon swimming.
Artist: William C. Morris, Alabama.
Print: 20,400 standard edition, 11,500 special edition.
Stamp: Face value, $7.50. Number printed, unavailable; number sold, 1,913,509. Money raised, $14,351,131.

1985–86

Title and medium: "Cinnamon Teal"; opaque watercolor.
Species and setting: A single drake cinnamon teal against a simple background of water and reeds.
Artist: Gerald Mobley, Oklahoma.
Print: Three editions: 18,200-print standard edition, 6,650 medallion edition and 6,650 edition with companion piece.
Stamp: Face value, $7.50. Number printed, unavailable; number sold, 1,779,299. Money raised, $13,344,742.

1986–87

Title and medium: "Fulvous Whistling Duck"; acrylic.
Species and setting: A single fulvous whistling duck, an unusual southern species, swimming away from the viewer.
Artist: Burton E. Moore Jr., South Carolina.
Print: 16,310 standard edition, plus a 4,670 medallion edition.
Stamp: Face value, $7.50. Number printed, approximately 4,000,000; number sold, 1,793,383. Money raised, $17,933,830.
Notes: This was the first time this beautiful species of duck was featured on the federal stamp.

1987–88

Title: "Redheads".
Species and setting: Two drake redheads and a single hen sweep in low for a landing in a wooded cove.
Artist: Arthur G. Anderson, Wisconsin.
Print: 20,000 standard prints, plus a 5,000-print medallion edition.
Stamp: Face value, $10. Number printed, 4,000,000; number sold,

1,661,183. Money raised, $16,611,830.
Notes: Reacting to a string of winning designs that showed waterfowl sitting quietly, U.S. Fish and Wildlife instructed its judges to give priority to entries that showed life and action.

1988–89

Title: "Snow Goose".
Species and setting: A single adult snow goose flying across a lake at dawn.
Artist: Daniel Smith, Minnesota.
Print: 20,000 standard edition, plus 6,200 medallion and 750 solid gold medallion prints.
Stamp: Face value, $10. Number sold (partial figure through June 1989), 1,357,018. Money raised during same period, $13,570,180.

1989–90

Title and medium: "Lesser Scaup"; gouache.
Species and setting: Two lesser scaup swimming among reeds.
Artist: Neal R. Anderson, Nebraska.
Print: Information unavailable.
Stamp: Face value, $12.50. Stamp to go on sale July 1, 1989.
Notes: This was the first year the price of a stamp jumped above $10. It was also the first year in which the artists were restricted to a limited selection of species – lesser scaup, spectacled eider, red-breasted merganser, Barrow's goldeneye and black-bellied whistling duck. None of the five had ever appeared on a federal stamp.

Index